THE TRUE STELLA AWARDS

Praise for Randy Cassingham and StellaAwards.com

"How did [Cassingham] get so popular so fast? Well, for one thing, he writes funny stuff."

—*The New York Times*

"Stella Awards [are the] Oscars for creative litigation."

—*The Guardian* (London)

"Cassingham has no trouble finding loony lawsuits. Lawyers have convinced Americans that every time something bad happens, someone has to pay—even if that someone was not at fault."

—*The Star-Ledger* (Newark)

"The name Stella has become shorthand for an outrageous or ridiculous lawsuit. StellaAwards.com honors those who spectacularly misuse the legal system."

—*Playboy*

"Cassingham's true cases of lawsuit abuse are almost as outrageous as the made-up ones."

—*The Macon Telegraph*

"[Cassingham] has a keen eye for life's bizarre twists. . . . Cassingham is a humorist for the information age, an Internet-savvy satirist and social commentator. The Jay Leno of cyberspace."

—*Los Angeles Times*

THE TRUE STELLA AWARDS

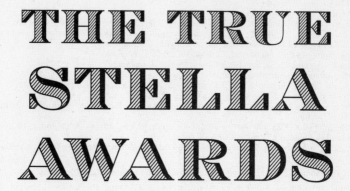

Honoring Real Cases of Greedy Opportunists, Frivolous Lawsuits, and the Law Run Amok

RANDY CASSINGHAM

A PLUME BOOK

PLUME
Published by Penguin Group
Penguin Group (USA) Inc., 375 Hudson Street, New York, New York 10014, U.S.A.
Penguin Group (Canada), 90 Eglinton Avenue East, Suite 700, Toronto, Ontario, Canada M4P 2Y3 (a division of Pearson Penguin Canada Inc.)
Penguin Books Ltd., 80 Strand, London WC2R 0RL, England
Penguin Ireland, 25 St. Stephen's Green, Dublin 2, Ireland
(a division of Penguin Books Ltd.)
Penguin Group (Australia), 250 Camberwell Road, Camberwell, Victoria 3124, Australia (a division of Pearson Australia Group Pty. Ltd.)
Penguin Books India Pvt. Ltd., 11 Community Centre, Panchsheel Park, New Delhi – 110 017, India
Penguin Books (NZ), cnr Airborne and Rosedale Roads, Albany, Auckland 1310, New Zealand (a division of Pearson New Zealand Ltd.)
Penguin Books (South Africa) (Pty.) Ltd., 24 Sturdee Avenue, Rosebank, Johannesburg 2196, South Africa

Penguin Books Ltd., Registered Offices: 80 Strand, London WC2R 0RL, England

Published by Plume, a member of Penguin Group (USA) Inc. Previously published in a Dutton edition.

First Plume Printing, November 2006
10 9 8 7 6 5 4 3 2

The Library of Congress has catalogued the Dutton edition as follows:
Cassingham, R. C. (Randy C.)
True Stella awards / by Randy Cassingham.
p. cm.
ISBN 0-525-94913-5 (hc.)
ISBN 0-452-28771-5 (pbk.)
1. Frivolous suits (Civil procedure)—United States. 2. Law—United States—Humor. I. Title.
KF8887.C37 2005
347. 73'53—dc22   2005011382

Printed in the United States of America
Original hardcover design by Virginia Norey

PUBLISHER'S NOTE

Contents

4. It's Not My Responsibility

5. Petty Squabbles

6. It's My Right!
The Infinite Expansion of the Constitution 127

7. It Ought to Be a Crime
Lawsuits by Inmates and Criminals 157

8. The Class-Action Lottery
The Queue Forms Here 171

9. School Daze
What Are Our Kids Really Learning? 187

THE TRUE STELLA AWARDS

Genesis
The Birth of the Stella Awards

The True Stella Awards recognize the most frivolous civil lawsuits filed in the United States. Such as the diabetic obese man with high blood pressure and heart disease who sued the fast-food industry for not telling him that it just might not be healthy for him to eat at McDonald's every day, as if having two heart attacks weren't enough to convince him. Such as the lawyer who had a pet nonprofit he wanted to get publicity for, so he "sued Oreo cookies." Such as the guy who had his name legally changed to Jack Ass—and then sued because the TV show and movie *Jackass* somehow disparaged his good name.

And yes, all of those cases are real, and are featured in these pages.

Most people simply blame lawyers, which only recognizes part of the real problem. The True Stella Awards are not a campaign against lawyers. Most lawyers are good and decent people who are trying to do the best they can for their clients and the ideals of justice. On the other hand, some of their peers just don't get it, and defend even their most outrageous actions by claiming, "Everybody hates lawyers until they need one." That's not true at all:

Most people hate lawyers even then. The problem is that we *need* lawyers. People can't simply and reasonably explain their cases to the court and expect judges or juries to hand down decisions based on reason or logic—or even common sense. The American legal system has been so manipulated and convoluted by lawyers that we need them to navigate our way through the complexities of the legal system—complexities they themselves created. People need doctors, too, but we don't hate them as a profession because doctors are not in the business of curing diseases that they themselves created.

Is that fair? You bet. Lawsuits can accurately be called an industry in the United States. The lawsuit industry is estimated to bring in more than $50 billion per year in legal fees to lawyers out of over $250 billion in total cost to the litigants (2004 estimate). That's a huge drain on the country's economy: It represents well over 2 percent of the U.S. gross domestic product. By comparison, the United Kingdom's "lawsuit load" is less than 1 percent of its GDP.

And it's a growing industry. As of 2001 (the most recent year that data is available), the thirty-year trends are: U.S. population, up at a 1.1 percent annual rate; the consumer price index, up 5 percent annually; the GDP, up 7.6 percent annually. And tort costs? Up 9.1 percent annually—and they were up by 14.3 percent in 2001. This industry's growth is not only staggering, it's accelerating.

What Is a "Tort"?

"Tort" is most easily explained as a civil wrong. Robbery is a crime; being injured by a defective product is a tort. Crimes are dealt with in criminal courts after a suspect is indicted; torts are dealt with in civil courts after a defendant is sued. A tort can be accidental or intentional; when intentional, for example an assault, it may also be prosecuted as a crime.

The purpose of the tort system is twofold: to compensate people for their injuries (physical, financial, etc.) and to provide incentive to people and companies to work to reduce injury to others—because they don't want to be sued. But just like a police state can go way overboard, ruling by intimidation, the tort system can also get out of hand, ruling by fear and destroying the economic incentive to produce goods, help someone in need, etc. Most "tort reform" organizations would argue that the tort system is already out of balance.

And that $50 billion figure is for lawsuit income only; it does not include anything else lawyers do, doesn't include any collected percentage of punitive damages, and doesn't even include their take from the "tobacco settlement," for which the eighty-six law firms involved have billed the states a whopping $30 billion. But don't say they don't have a heart: They're graciously allowing the states to pay those fees over twenty-five years. And some of those firms say they've been ripped off, that they deserve much more! Yet when you divide the billings of one firm by the total estimated hours they spent working on this one case, it comes out to more than $22,000 per hour! Other firms are "only" getting around $10,000 per hour. And you know they're billing for plenty of hours.

So at least one segment of the U.S. economy is booming even while as a whole Americans are struggling. One thing to ponder: Perhaps that's a cause-and-effect situation.

In a "Background and Need for the Legislation" report to support the Attorney Accountability Act of 1995 (which, as you may have noticed, wasn't passed), the U.S. House of Representatives pointed out that in 1989, eighteen million lawsuits were filed in the country's state and federal courts, or one lawsuit per ten citizens. Court dockets were so full that in 1990, more than 10 percent of all federal cases were still pending three years after they were filed, leading to the reality that "justice is often delayed and as a result is often denied." The report noted that federal court caseloads were expected to double every fourteen years.

Obviously, not all lawsuits are frivolous; probably the majority are reasonable. But a growing number of cases *are* frivolous. As you're about to see, the cases featured here span from the merely humorous to the absolutely outrageous. You'll wonder how any lawyer, any court, any jury could entertain such cases, let alone pay the idiot plaintiffs big money.

But before that, you might just wonder: Who the heck is Stella?

Stella!

Few recognize the name Stella Liebeck, but when I'm talking to people and say she's the lady who spilled Mc-

Donald's coffee in her lap and then sued the restaurant—
and won—every single American I have ever told, without
exception, says something along the lines of, "Oh, yeah,
her!" Everyone seems to know about the woman who sued
McDonald's, but few know more than the most elemental
aspects of her case.

In 1992, Stella, then 79, spilled a cup of McDonald's coffee onto her lap, burning herself, and then sued over her
injuries. A New Mexico jury awarded her $2.9 million in
damages. During the trial, a number of points were made
by her attorneys—and by the lawyers representing the
restaurant—but few have ever heard the whole story behind her lawsuit. Consider these details:

* Stella was not driving when she pulled the lid off her
  scalding McDonald's coffee. Her grandson was driving
  the car, and he had pulled over to stop so she could add
  cream and sugar to the cup. So she was not only not driving, but the car was not moving.

* Stella was burned badly—6 to 16 percent of her skin was
  burned, and she needed treatment and rehabilitation, including skin grafts, over a two-year span. McDonald's refused an offer to settle with her for $20,000 in medical
  costs.

* McDonald's quality control managers specified that its
  coffee should be served at 180 to 190 degrees Fahrenheit.
  Liquids at that temperature can cause third-degree burns
  in two to seven seconds. Such burns require skin graft-
  ing, debridement, and whirlpool treatments to heal, and
  the resulting scarring is typically permanent.

✳ From 1982 to 1992, McDonald's coffee burned more than seven hundred people, usually slightly but sometimes seriously, resulting in some other claims and lawsuits.

✳ Witnesses for McDonald's admitted in court that consumers are unaware of the extent of the risk of serious burns from spilled coffee served at McDonald's required temperature, admitted that it did not warn customers of this risk, could offer no explanation as to why it did not, and testified that it did not intend to turn down the heat even though it admitted that its coffee is "not fit for consumption" when sold because it is too hot.

✳ While Stella was awarded $200,000 in compensatory damages, this amount was reduced by 20 percent (to $160,000) because the jury found her 20 percent at fault. Where did the rest of the $2.9 million figure in? The jury awarded her $2.7 million in punitive damages, based on two days of McDonald's coffee sales—but the judge later reduced that amount to $480,000, or three times the "actual" damages that were awarded.

But wait . . .

✳ The resulting $640,000 isn't the end, either. Liebeck and McDonald's entered into secret settlement negotiations rather than go to appeal. The amount of the settlement is not known—it's secret!

✳ The plaintiffs were apparently able to document seven hundred cases of burns from McDonald's coffee over ten years, or seventy burns per year. That sounds impressive, but that includes *every* sort of burn, from Stella's serious scalding to minor skin redness. It also doesn't take into account how many cups were sold without incident: A McDonald's consultant pointed out the seven hundred cases in ten years represents just one injury per *twenty-four million* cups sold. For every injury, no matter how severe, 23,999,999 people managed to drink their coffee without any injury whatever. Isn't that sufficient proof right there that McDonald's coffee is not "unreasonably dangerous"?

* Even in the eyes of an obviously sympathetic jury, Stella was judged to be 20 percent at fault—she did, after all, spill the coffee into her lap all by herself. The car was stopped, so she presumably was not bumped to cause the spill. Indeed, she chose to hold the coffee cup between her knees instead of any number of safer locations as she opened it. Should she have taken more responsibility for her own actions?

And . . .

* Here's the kicker: Coffee is *supposed* to be served in the range of 185 degrees! The National Coffee Association recommends coffee be brewed at "between 195–205 degrees Fahrenheit for optimal extraction" and drunk "immediately." If not drunk immediately, it should be "maintained at 180–185 degrees Fahrenheit" (*Source*: NCAUSA Web site). Exactly what, then, did McDonald's do wrong? Did it exhibit "willful, wanton, reckless or malicious conduct"—the standard in New Mexico for awarding punitive damages?

Clearly America's "Court of Public Opinion" doesn't think so, but Stella indeed won her case, sparking the imagination of everyone who heard about it. As her fame spread, the Court of Public Opinion issued its own verdict: Stella has become an American icon, a symbol of the American tort system gone wrong. Most people have not only heard of her case, they have an opinion on it.

Probably because of that already existing notoriety, an unknown someone, probably on the Internet, applied the name "Stella Award" to any wild, outrageous, or ridiculous lawsuit. Then something happened—something that the Internet not only fosters, but helps spread: The concept of the "Stella Awards" became a *meme*. Someone—and no one really knows who—produced a tightly written summary of a number of American lawsuits and the runners-up and, ultimately, the winner, of the "most ridiculous lawsuit of the year." That e-mail has been going around (and around and around!) by e-mail ever since. Usually, the roundup leads off with this one:

> *Kathleen Robertson of Austin, Texas, was awarded $780,000 by a jury after breaking her ankle tripping over a toddler who was running amok inside a furniture store. The owners of the store were understandably surprised at the verdict, considering the misbehaving tyke was Ms. Robertson's son.*

The problem: No courts around Austin have ever heard of Ms. Robertson, and there is no record of such a case being filed, let alone won.

> *Carl Truman, 19, of Los Angeles won $74,000 and medical expenses when his neighbor ran his hand over with a*

*Honda Accord. Mr. Truman apparently didn't notice some-
one was at the wheel of the car whose hubcap he was trying
to steal.*

Never happened. It's not a legal case; it sounds more
like it's part of a comedian's patter.

*A Philadelphia restaurant was ordered to pay Amber Car-
son of Lancaster, Pennsylvania, $113,500 after she slipped
on a spilled soft drink and broke her coccyx. The beverage
was on the floor because Ms. Carson threw it at her boy-
friend thirty seconds earlier during an argument.*

Completely fabricated.

*In November 2000, Mr. Grazinski purchased a brand-
new thirty-two-foot Winnebago motor home. On his first trip
home, having joined the freeway, he set the cruise control at
seventy miles per hour and calmly left the driver's seat to go
into the back and make himself a cup of coffee. Not surprisingly, the Winnie left the freeway, crashed, and overturned.
Mr. Grazinski sued Winnebago for not advising him in the
handbook that he could not actually do this. He was awarded
$1,750,000 plus a new Winnebago.*

You guessed it: It's fake. In fact, *all* of the cases in the
popular e-mail are fake. They never happened. They're urban legends.

The "Mr. Grazinski" case is the ultimate Fake Stella
Award—it's the winning case every year. You'd think that
the same case being presented as the "winner" year after
year would clue people in to the fact that the whole thing
is a gag, yet people forward the batch of cases, these and

several others, again and again with the same "ain't it awful?!" introduction. And the only thing that changes on the made-up Stella Awards urban legend e-mail is the supposed year that these cases came to trial so they could be in the running as the "winner" of the Stella Award for that year.

With an unusual name like "Grazinski" and a specific company involved, it should be easy to locate the case, right? Right—if it's real. But it's not. Winnebago Industries is so tired of the story that they posted a notice on their Web site saying it's untrue so people will stop writing them to ask, and they link to the True Stella Awards in an attempt to reduce the number of inquiries on the subject. As the supposed defendant who paid out "$1,750,000 plus a new Winnebago," they ought to know the truth behind it. And the truth is, it's a fictitious story. A fake. A gag. Still, despite the earmarks of an urban legend, thousands still think it's true; they believe our court system is broken enough for it to be plausible. And sadly, when you think of it that way, it *is* plausible, even if it's not true, so they forward the e-mail to their friends, doing their part to keep the meme alive.

And that's why this book is called the *True* Stella Awards: The ones I write up are *actual* cases. So why did I go to the trouble?

Turning Fiction into Reality

I've been writing an online newspaper column on weird-but-true news called *This is True* since 1994. I allow readers to submit stories for the column, and you guessed it: I get more submissions of the so-called Stella Awards—the urban legend case write-ups—than anything else. My readers perceive a problem with lawsuit abuse and want me to write more about it. But what's the point in illustrating an actual problem using falsified evidence? Besides, my column is called *This is True*, and I'm not about to stain my trademark by featuring faked cases.

Then I found out that trial lawyers were using the existence of the widely distributed urban legend Stella Awards to "prove" that there was no problem with runaway legal abuse. "People wouldn't have to make up these fake cases if there were real ones to illustrate the so-called problem," their theory went. Those were fighting words! After years of weekly research to find stupid people doing stupid things to feature in *This is True*, I knew there were plenty of actual frivolous lawsuits I could write about. If nothing else, I had years of story archives I could draw on. So I started a new feature called the True Stella Awards to help counter the urban legends.

The point isn't to debunk urban legends, but rather to show that there are real cases of the abuse of our civil courts. A guy putting his Winnebago on autopilot and going to the back to make coffee (why is it so often coffee?) is entertaining, to be sure, but it doesn't advance the public discussion that needs to take place about lawsuits. That doesn't mean real cases can't be funny, though, as Mr. Jack Ass so ably proved.

But a funny thing happened on the way to publication: I never had to dig into my "weird news" archives. I was always able to find recent cases to write about. Trial lawyers claim that there are no real cases to discuss? The True Stella Awards put the lie to that claim in a hurry.

I set up the StellaAwards.com Web site as a placeholder while I waited for my schedule to clear to launch it as a newsletter. There was some vague "coming soon" stuff on there, and a form where people could sign up for an e-mail distribution of cases when they were issued . . . without any promise of when that might be. Yet people signed up for the e-mail distribution at the rate of one per hour, and it increased from there as word spread—people were hungry for the truth on an important issue that was starting to affect the average person's life.

By the time the first True Stella Awards case write-up came out in September 2002, more than six thousand people had signed up to get it! By the end of that year more than twenty-five thousand people had subscribed. To a *legal case* newsletter written by a nonlawyer? Clearly there was hunger for real information on this issue.

"IANAL"

It's probably significant that I am not a lawyer ("IANAL," in online dialect), nor am I associated with any "tort reform" organization. Rather, I'm simply interested in provoking public discussion on a situation that I believe is causing great harm to society: the rampant abuse of the American civil court system. Once you read the cases, I hope you will not only agree, but will actively help work toward implementing a comprehensive solution to the mess; the last chapter talks about what can be done, even by the average person on the street—yes, even *you*. I'm not a lawyer, and you don't have to be, either, to have a real and positive impact on the problem.

Those in the legal profession don't always appreciate the public looking over its shoulder. One angry lawyer demanded of me, "Since when do *you* define what is appropriate for judicial determination?" Meaning, of course, that she considers her actions beyond the scope of review by mere citizens. Those actions are taken in the courts that belong to The People, where she is an officer sworn to protect and defend the country's courts "by, of, and for The People." Since the "People" are all of us, it necessarily follows that abuse of the court system is abuse of us all. And "We the People" are only just now starting to understand that the *costs* of lawsuits are being passed to us all. This lawyer forgets who she works for, yet she's far from the only lawyer with such an attitude, as you'll see later.

Happily, however, *most* lawyers are as angry with the system as we mere citizens are, and a significant percentage of the True Stella Awards' online readers are lawyers. They lament the damage done by a minority of their peers. Many got into law for idealistic reasons, and they learned, quickly and harshly, that there is little room for idealism in the real world of litigation—and that makes them angry. They, too, want to see reason and common sense return to the courtroom.

Where the Cases Come From

Rather than dig into the archives of my weird news *This is True* feature for cases, I started by researching to see if there was anything fresh to use. And sure enough, I always found *more* recent cases than I could possibly write about. Which pretty much goes to show that there really is a pervasive problem: It's *that* easy to find examples of silly lawsuits, even though I limit my discussion to cases filed in U.S. courts.

Since I'm not a lawyer or otherwise involved in the legal system, and because I wanted my readers to be able to see my sources and be able to judge each case's merits for themselves, I decided from the start that I would only use online sources for the cases—articles from mainstream, legitimate newspaper Web sites, legal news sites, and other such sources—so that readers could visit the same places where I got my information and judge for themselves whether my write-up was fair and representative of the facts. Occasionally I will find a progressive court that posts filed suits or decisions online, and I will use that material for details, but most people don't have the stomach to plow through the legalese. I thus prefer to rely on more layperson-friendly sources whenever possible, even though their treatment is sometimes more simplistic than a legal scholar would prefer.

This approach does have a negative side, however: Newspapers obviously cannot report every word of a case. Sometimes only one side wants to tell their story to the reporter, and obviously they tell the details that are favorable to them. In many cases, the parties will negotiate secret out-of-court settlements which, by their very nature, are kept from the public (which I decry, for reasons I'll explain later). And while newspapers love screaming headlines that announce a new multimillion-dollar case, they much less readily report on the less-than-spectacular denouement, or the reversal of a bad decision in an appeal. Thus, obviously, the summary case write-ups in this book are definitely not perfect, nor can they represent the whole picture. However, in many cases I have been able to get more details as time has gone by, and that follow-up information is included in an afterword below the case write-up. In rare instances the added information is enough to change my mind. In one instance I actually revoked the Stella Award given to a case after I learned a detail the newspaper didn't report. Rather than delete the case, I left it in so that readers could see the thought process behind the decision.

The most frequent question about my case write-ups is: "What happened?" Some of the cases are written up shortly after they've been decided, but I often feature cases that have just been filed. I also would like to know the "ultimate outcome" of these suits, but one of the other problems with our civil system is that the outcome is often not known for *many* years. Indeed, that's a tactic of some of the bullies involved in civil litigation: They prolong the case for years so their adversaries run out of the large amounts of money needed to pursue their claim. The typical TSA case, however, seems to take two to three years to be decided. Thus, for many cases featured here, that date (at the point this was written) is still in the future. The bottom line is, even winning lawsuits are hardly the get-rich-quick scheme many seem to think they are.

In other words, unlike the fantasy world of the urban legend Stella Awards, in real life the courts are so clogged, and "justice" so slow, that it can take many years for a case to conclude; "What happened?" just can't be answered. Sorry, but there are no pat endings in the real world.

It's also important to remember that the True Stella Awards are *not* about outrageous civil court *awards*, but rather civil court *abuse*; even when a case is quickly thrown out (and that doesn't happen often enough!), there is still a profound cumulative impact on the courts, on the defendants, and on society. When cases are thrown out, lawyers like to say, "See? There is no problem! The system worked!" Meanwhile, legitimate cases have to wait until the piles of garbage are cleared away to make room on the docket. "The system" may "work," but society is still broken.

Awareness Is Only the Start

Despite what many "tort reform" groups would have you believe, there is no easy solution to frivolous lawsuits. I will, however, conclude this book with some ideas to help further the social debate that started long before I entered the scene. And indeed, it will take a lengthy and in-depth dialogue among informed citizens and reform-minded insiders to carefully weigh the pros and cons of various approaches, and then slowly and carefully introduce reforms. But Band-Aid solutions, which have been proposed by various special interest reform groups and politicians, will not work. A top-to-bottom, systemic solution is needed, and such changes are never easy. But the rising chorus that led to, and is amplified by, this book will eventually force action.

In my case write-ups, by the way, there is no attempt to shield the guilty: I use the real names of the people involved. There's no point in discussing true cases and debunking made-up ones if I change the names, thus fictionalizing the truth.

Last, keep in mind: The cases in the True Stella Awards are . . . well . . . true. Remember to laugh; it helps to keep you from crying.

Agents of Change
Abusing the Courts to Further an Agenda

Some lawsuits aren't so much about damaged people seeking reparations as they are about using the courts as a way to further a personal or political agenda. But that's not really what the courts are there for, and when the docket is clogged up with silly grandstanding, cases with actual merit get pushed further and further into the future, delaying their justice. And as nineteenth-century British Prime Minister William Gladstone liked to say, "Justice delayed is justice denied."

```
1                   *              )   Location: Pennsylvania
                                   )
2        Fringe Religion           )   Year: 2004
                                   )
3              v.                  )   Award Status:
                                   )   Dishonorable Mention
4         "Reality" TV             )
                                   )
5    ----------------------------- )
```

THAT VOODOO YOU DO
NOT WELL

It might seem a bit strange that the SciFi cable TV channel might air a "reality" show—after all, the "Fi" stands for "Fiction"—but who ever said "reality TV" was an accurate depiction of life?

Be that as it may, *Mad Mad House* ran in 2004 on the SciFi Channel, which is owned by Universal Studios. Judging by its ratings you've probably never heard of the show, so here's the scoop, obtained from the SciFi Web site while it was still on the air:

Five practitioners of "alternative lifestyles"—a Wiccan, a Naturist, a Modern Primitive, a Voodoo Priestess and a real-life Vampire (known collectively as the Alts)—rule the roost. Meanwhile, 10 ordinary folks move into the House as the Alts' Guests—and compete against one another for the $100,000 jackpot. Our Guests will live out a Survivor *meets* The Real World *meets* The Osbournes *lifestyle—and try to get along living under one roof together. The eclectic and unpredictable Alts will challenge them, judge them and eliminate them one by one—ultimately deciding which Guest is most fit for life in the Mad Mad House.*

The show finished up in 2004, so I think it's OK to say the winning "Guest" was the stripper. Sorry, but it was against the rules to do the obvious: vote any of the weirdos . . . er, "Alts" . . . out of the house.

Of the five "Alts," which would you think might have been the most controversial? Perhaps the Naturist? (If you don't know the term, you probably know the more common "nudist.") But nope, that was just a silly yawn, thanks to strategically placed houseplants and such.

Well, how about the "Modern Primitive"? That would be Art, who practices "ritual suspension" (he likes to hang around) and "other traditions" that are "based on Native American rites of passage." Rather than live on a reservation in the middle of a southwestern desert, Art is "a professional piercing artist and body-modifier. His goal is to cover his own body with Polynesian and Marquesan art." In publicity photos, he doesn't seem to wear much more than "Avocado," the name that the naturist Alt, David Wolfe, prefers to go by. Rather, Art mainly sports geometric tattoos, even on his face. Nah—nothing out of the ordinary there.

Then there's Ta'Shia, the "Voodoo Priestess." OK, OK, this one was preshadowed by the case title. Yep: She's the controversial one. SciFi says Iya Ta'Shia Asanti was raised Christian, but "later became disenchanted with it." So she "embraced the tenets of Voodoo and has spent more than a decade studying and training in the field of African spirituality. She is a co-founder of the Ifa Conference on African Spiritual Tradition, a priestess of Yemoja in the Ifa tradition, a civil-rights activist, a teacher of African traditions and culture," and—wait for it!—"an award-winning poet." The point of her being on the show was to educate people that voodoo is "a sacred religion unlike the misrepresentations popularized in entertainment."

Sounds like a reasonable goal. But not to the National African Religion Congress, Inc., which likes to be called NARC. Based not in Africa but in Philadelphia, NARC said depicting Ta'Shia as a voodoo priestess "demeans and misrepresents the voodoo religion."

"People already have negative feelings about this religion without a program like this exacerbating things," said NARC president George Ware before the program had even aired.

Since the NARCs hadn't seen the show yet, they had to go by its advertising and publicity to criticize it. At the time they said Ta'Shia does not wear the correct clothing for a voodoo priestess, and that the promotional clips for the show depict her doing things that aren't part of the religion. God (or whoever) forbid!

So the self-proclaimed "African" group embraced the American way: It filed a lawsuit in federal court against Universal Studios, USA Cable Entertainment, and show producer House of Eleven Productions demanding that the court order the show to change its advertising and programming. The suit says Ta'Shia isn't a voodoo priestess, but rather merely a priestess of "Yemoja in the Ifa tradition." Thus, the SciFi Channel must be forced to stop calling Ta'Shia a voodoo priestess, and be restrained from "airing any episode . . . that falsely portrays any practice of African-based religions."

Perhaps unwittingly, the lawsuit reveals a possible ulterior motive: It says the show's producers signed Ta'Shia for the show only after failing to sign Gro Mambo Angela Novanyon, "a recognized Haitian voodoo high priestess in Philadelphia." And just who is she? She happens to be the founder of NARC.

But two months after filing the suit, NARC dropped it. In its newsletter, NARC noted the suit was settled when SciFi agreed to put a disclaimer on the *Mad Mad House* Web site. "The relief NARC sought in its suit," the newsletter noted, "i.e., an injunction blocking broadcast of the show, was not possible because of First Amendment protections given to free speech." Darn those pesky American freedoms! And, um, didn't they know about that basic right before they filed suit? (Of course they did; that's not the point. Publicity and pressure was.) Although they admitted they had no legal leg to stand on, NARC still ominously hinted that "other relief may be sought in the future" now that the lawsuit has fallen on its face.

Meanwhile, right through to the end, the show's Web site still billed Ta'Shia as a "Voodoo Priestess." (What a shock!) Let's hope the suits in SciFi's executive suite didn't injure themselves when they rolled their eyes—that could be an actionable injury.

The bottom line here is, who is SciFi to judge whether someone is a priest or priestess? It's not like they can call Rome and check the credentials of a voodoo practitioner. There is certainly no organization with a proprietary right to the term "voodoo." If Ta'Shia wants to be known as a "Voodoo Priestess," why *shouldn't* the producers take her word for it? For them to insist she be labeled in a different way, indeed, could be considered religious discrimination.

Ironically, in the same issue of their newsletter NARC editorialized against "Holier Than Thou Disease," lamenting that "the National African Religion Congress constantly encounters dissension from one spiritual house to another and from one African-based religion to another." In the editorial, Gro Mambo Angela Novanyon herself lectured that "it takes a small mind and a lack of spiritual education to think that your religion is the purest, most powerful, and the only religion recognized by God."

Voodoo practitioners: Heal yourselves!

Sources:

* "Suit: TV Show Demeans Voodoo," *Philadelphia Inquirer,* 24 February 2004
* NARC Web site: http://www.NARCworld.com
* *Mad Mad House* Web site: http://www.scifi.com/madmad house/

Who Do Voodoo?

More than sixty million people practice voodoo worldwide. (*Source: ReligiousTolerance.org*)

1	*	) Location: California
2	Special Interest Group	) Year: 2003
3	Needing Publicity	) Award Status: Runner-up
4	v.	) for the 2003 Stella Award
5	Oreo Cookies	)

TRANS-FRIVOLOUS
LAWSUIT

After reading several articles about "trans fatty acids," which are a product of the partially hydrogenated oils used in many foods, San Francisco attorney Stephen Joseph became concerned. The articles, among the three thousand articles that have been printed in various publications since 1993, said that trans fats are "hidden" in many snack foods. Trans fats are thought to increase cholesterol and cause other health problems. The National Academy of Sciences' Institute of Medicine recently linked trans fats with heart disease and said that they cannot be consumed safely in any amount; clearly, then, they are a reasonable cause for alarm.

Based on these growing concerns, the U.S. Food and Drug Administration ruled that food manufacturers must list trans fats on the standard nutritional information labels. But because food manufacturers are fighting the rule, it was still pending as attorney Joseph was getting more and more upset.

One of the many thousands of products that contain

trans fats: Oreo cookies—the best-selling cookies in the United States. Joseph decided that Oreo cookies were so dangerous he filed a lawsuit in Superior Court in Marin County, California, seeking an injunction forbidding Kraft Foods, owner of Oreo maker Nabisco, from selling the snack to children in California.

The lawsuit, based on a California law that holds manufacturers liable for unsafe products if it's not "common knowledge" that the product is unsafe, didn't target any other foods, even though about 40 percent of *all* foods include trans fats, including cookies, crackers, and other processed foods.

"Tobacco is well known as an unsafe product. Trans fat is not the same thing at all. Very few people know about it," Joseph said after filing his suit. "That's why [my] trans fat [lawsuit] is a far stronger case than tobacco or [cases against] McDonald's," he reasoned, "because people know those are dangerous."

In addition to his suit, Joseph started a nonprofit group whose goal it is to ban trans fats, and printed T-shirts that say "Don't Partially Hydrogenate Me." The group's Web site recorded record traffic after articles about Joseph's lawsuit hit the newspapers.

"Anything that brings people's attention to how dangerous and unhealthy trans fat can be is probably a good idea," said California State Senator Debra Bowen, who is known for nutrition-reform legislation. *Anything*, Senator Bowen? Be careful what you ask for. The publicity resulting from Joseph's lawsuit was intense: Articles about "suing Oreos" ran all over the world. In fact, Joseph said, he got so much publicity for his cause and Web site that he dropped his lawsuit just thirteen days after he filed it.

"You've got to recognize when you've scored a home

run," Joseph said. "We have raised the awareness of trans fat to the top of the mountain. What more success do I want? To force Kraft to crawl? Kraft is going to have to deal with the fact that the public is now aware of what it puts in Oreos."

Senator Bowen was unhappy with Joseph dropping the suit. "To see someone file a suit, then drop it after they've decided they've gotten enough media attention for it, is pretty disappointing," she said. "A stunt like this does more harm than good because people will walk away from it thinking since the suit was a joke, then any claims about trans fat being dangerously unhealthy for them must be a joke, too."

Meanwhile, Kraft Foods said it only got 277 calls or e-mails about Oreos after the suit hit, and about half of those supported the company. Only 15 percent were "critical" of the company. The rest merely wanted more information.

Still, Joseph considered the suit a success. "At the time the lawsuit was filed nobody knew about trans fat. Now everybody knows," he said.

A spokesman for Kraft Foods said the company "doesn't believe that the courts are the place to make nutrition policy. That's best handled by nutrition professionals and regulatory agencies." He noted that the company was never served with the suit.

Is that the function of the civil courts in the U.S.? To drive publicity for special interest groups? To say "nobody knew" about trans fats ignores the three thousand articles that have been printed in the last decade, and ignores the fact that the FDA is already working to increase public awareness of the issue on nutrition labels. If awareness is at "the top of the mountain," the "mountain" must be made of the thousands of articles and regulatory actions that preceded Joseph's suit. And if the public was "not aware" of trans fats after ten years of articles, how does a couple of weeks of publicity about a frivolous lawsuit help? Obviously, it doesn't—but it does serve to drive traffic to Joseph's Web site, though only at the cost of further clogging up the courts so action on real issues is further delayed.

Food manufacturers have a duty to ensure that consumers are informed of relevant aspects of nutritional values so they can make intelligent decisions about what they buy and eat. That's exactly what the FDA is working toward, if slowly, and it's not to the manufacturers' credit that they fought the FDA's action to require trans fat labeling. But that doesn't make the issue worthy of court time.

As officers of the court, attorneys are supposed to be gatekeepers to keep frivolous lawsuits *out* of the system, not file them themselves for selfish reasons. That Kraft was never even served with the suit—and note how quickly it was dropped—suggests Joseph had no intention to have the court issue rulings on the case, or to entertain Kraft's legal response. Why wasn't Joseph censured by the State Bar for his outrageous exploitation of the courts by using the legal process as a publicity tool for his own special interest group? Even when faced with such obvious abuse, most courts still do nothing to sanction the parties involved. So Joseph got his way, got his publicity, and others are put on notice: A lawsuit is a cost-effective way to get quick publicity without generating repercussions.

Sources:

* ✳ "Lawsuit Seeks to Ban Sale of Oreos to Children in California," *San Francisco Chronicle,* 12 May 2003
* ✳ "S.F. Lawyer Plans to Drop Oreo Suit," *San Francisco Chronicle,* 15 May 2003
* ✳ "S.F. Lawyer Says He's Dropping Suit Against Oreo Cookies," Associated Press, 14 May 2003

Oreos

Oreos are the number-one-selling cookie in America, with sales of about half a billion dollars per year. (*Source: BakingBusiness.com*)

```
1                    *           )   Location: California
2            One Mom             )   Year: 2002
                                 )
3              v.                )   Award Status:
4       A Village Full of        )   Dishonorable Mention
                                 )
5          Parents               )
                                 )
```

ACTIVISTS ATTEMPT TO HOG-TIE PARENTS

City children often have no idea where meat comes from—farm and ranch life is just not part of their experience. In an effort to bring the country to city kids, several schools in the San Francisco Bay Area sponsor field trips to the Cow Palace in San Francisco for Grand National Rodeo Day, where they can see animal exhibits and, yes, a rodeo. The field trips have been going on for twenty years and have been so successful they were recently expanded. About nine thousand students were expected to attend in 2002.

The schoolchildren "not only see a rodeo," said Cow Palace CEO Michael Wegher, "but they see horse show events, working sheep dog trials, precision drill teams. It's a great chance for children who maybe couldn't afford a ticket, or perhaps their families don't have the time, to see the Western heritage."

But not if Peggy Hilden has anything to say about it.

Hilden sued on behalf of her son, asking the San Francisco Superior Court to stop schools from sending chil-

dren to the Cow Palace. The suit claims that "students witness men causing pain to frightened animals," and in the
past twenty years "at least seven" animals were injured in
the rodeo and either died or had to be put down—about
one every three years. The suit does not allege that any
schoolchildren saw any of the deaths.

Hilden's suit, which was also joined by the groups "In
Defense of Animals" and "Action for Animals," claims that
it has a legal foundation: The California Education Code,
the lawsuit says, prohibits schools "from teaching and encouraging inhumane treatment of animals" and, it claims,
steer wrestling, calf roping, bull riding, and other common rodeo events are all just that. The suit names school
districts in Alameda, Santa Clara, San Francisco, and San
Mateo Counties, accusing them all of violating the Education Code.

Nonsense, said Wegher of the Cow Palace. "The animals
are not abused," he said. "Some of those animals are better
cared for than some people in the world." He noted that a
bull was killed in 2000, but not when schoolkids were in
the audience. "It wasn't intentional," he said. "It's like driving on the freeway—sometimes accidents happen."

Attorney David Blatte, who drafted the suit, said the
"violence" that children "may" see at the rodeo "could upset" them. He knew his suit was filed too late to stop the
2002 event. "So the goal," he admitted, "is to at least stop
them next year."

In the Old West, parents were responsible for their children, and for teaching them right and wrong. That's why
the schools ask them to decide whether their children
should attend the rodeo, and give their permission in writing. But in the New West, a child's upbringing is up to
lawyers and nosy activists with an agenda; parents can get

the heck out of the way. Peggy Hilden seems to think that these days, it takes a court—not a village—to raise a child.

Source:

* "Suit: Rodeo Bad for Kids," *San Jose Mercury News,* 23 October 2002

Afterword:

The online readers' reaction to this case was rather interesting. Impassioned letters about rites of passage, the heritage of the West, how wonderful rodeo is. Impassioned letters about animal cruelty, injuries to animals and humans, and how awful rodeo is. Both extremes totally and completely missed the point.

It should be up to each kid's parents to decide whether or not their children should go see the rodeo, which was offered to area schools free of charge. And that's *exactly* what the schools were doing: asking the parents to decide. But the woman who sued wasn't content with that—she wanted to decide for those parents, as if they couldn't decide correctly, and chose to abuse the courts to force her values on others no matter what the parents' feelings were on the matter. The case wasn't about the rodeo; it was about using the courts to force a personal agenda on others. Or, rather, *abusing* the court to further a pet issue.

In July 2003, a San Francisco judge dismissed the charges against all the school districts except San Francisco, because that's where Hilden pays taxes. In 2004, the judge granted summary judgment to the school district, denied a motion from the plaintiffs for reconsideration, and ordered that the plaintiffs pay the school district's costs. Elapsed time from start to finish: more than a year.

```
1              *              )   Location: Not noted in
2      A Dead American       )   newspaper reports
3         Composer           )   Year: 2002
                             )
4            v.              )   Award Status:
5   Live British Musician    )   Dishonorable Mention
                             )
```

SILENCE IS GOLDEN—
IF YOU OWN IT

British musician Mike Batt produced the album *Classical Graffiti* for the rock group The Planets. The album had two distinct styles on it, so Batt decided to put a minute's break between the two sections.

"I thought for my own amusement it would be funny to call it something, so I called it 'A Minute's Silence' and credited it as track thirteen, and put my name as Batt/Cage, as a tongue-in-cheek dig at the John Cage piece," Batt said.

The Cage piece he referred to is a 1952 "composition" called "4'33"," a "famous" bit of "music"—four minutes and thirty-three seconds of silence—by American avant-garde composer John Cage, who died in 1992. Oddly, Cage was granted a copyright for "4'33" "—a copyright for, essentially, nothing. Batt's acknowledging Cage's "work," even in a cheeky way, was a big mistake: Peters Edition, Cage's music publisher, sued Batt for copyright infringement on behalf of the John Cage Trust, asking for a quarter of the royalties from Batt's album.

That's right: The lawsuit claims Batt stole his silence from Cage.

"As my mother said, 'Which bit of his four minutes and 33 seconds are they claiming you stole?' " Batt said at the time. None of it, he insisted. "I certainly wasn't quoting his silence. I claim my silence is original silence." Perhaps in the world of lawsuits such a claim makes some sort of logical sense.

When the infringement claim came to light, few thought it could possibly prevail. Duncan Lamont, a British lawyer specializing in the music industry, was one expert who rolled his eyes over the squabble. "Is [Cage's composition] a work? Has it been written down, is it a literary, artistic or dramatic work? The argument will be there is no work because there are no notes." If there is "no work," there could be no infringement and the case would fail.

Batt, too, was feisty. "Has the world gone mad? I'm prepared to do time rather than pay out," he told the press. "We are talking as much as 100,000 pounds" (U.S. $155,000) in royalties. Besides, he said, "mine is a much better silent piece. I have been able to say in one minute what Cage could only say in four minutes and thirty-three seconds."

But just a few months later, Batt was done—he settled out of court for an undisclosed six-figure sum, or pretty much what he was afraid he would have to pay if the suit succeeded. He handed over a check on the steps of the High Court in London, saying he was "making this gesture of a payment to the John Cage Trust in recognition of my own personal respect for John Cage and in recognition of his brave and sometimes outrageous approach to artistic experimentation in music."

A spokesman for Peters Edition, Cage's publisher, called the payment a "donation," which was accepted "in good spirit." He said the company had been ready to go to court to defend the copyright they controlled.

Donation, publicity stunt—or extortion payment? You be the judge, but be warned: Now that you know of this case, you really can't afford to be silent about it.

Sources:

* " 'Silent Works' Do Battle," BBC News Online, 17 July 2002
* "Mike Batt Sued over Copyright to Song of Silence," *Ananova*, 18 July 2002
* "British Musician to Pay in Lawsuit," Associated Press, 24 September 2002

 **Copyrights**

The U.S. Copyright Office, a division of the Library of Congress, receives about 607,000 applications for copyright registration each year. Only around 10 percent of the applications are rejected. (*Source: Library of Congress*)

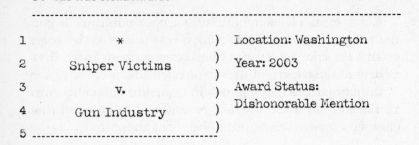

```
1            *             )  Location: Washington
                           )
2     Sniper Victims       )  Year: 2003
                           )
3            v.            )  Award Status:
                           )  Dishonorable Mention
4     Gun Industry         )
                           )
5   ------------------------)
```

TAKING DEAD AIM

After the Washington, D.C., area "Beltway Snipers" were caught, the public search effort turned its attentions elsewhere: for deep pockets to endow the bank accounts of the victims and their families.

The Brady Center to Prevent Gun Violence in Washington, D.C., in concert with a Seattle law firm, filed suit in Pierce County (Washington) Superior Court on behalf of two of the victims' families against Bushmaster Firearms, Inc., the manufacturer of the rifle used in the shootings, and the Tacoma, Washington, gun store the rifle was apparently stolen from. The Brady Center said other family members were "expected" to join the suit, if not file their own separate actions.

Attorney Paul Luvera said his "groundbreaking lawsuit" was absolutely not an attack on the rights of lawful gun owners or the Second Amendment of the Constitution. The gun manufacturer disagreed. "This lawsuit is really an attempt by the well-financed anti-gun groups there to push their agenda," said a Bushmaster spokesman. "It's an intentionally frivolous lawsuit," agreed the gun store's attorney, "designed more for publicity than substance."

Guns have plenty of lawful purposes; how is a gun manufacturer liable for the *illegal* misuse of their *stolen* product? The actions of Bushmaster and Bull's Eye Shooter Supply constitute a "public nuisance," says the suit. According to that theory they should have also sued Chevrolet, since the automaker did nothing—nothing at all—to stop the murderers from drilling a hole in the trunk lid of their Caprice sedan to convert it into a mobile sniper's nest.

But despite the contention that the suit was "designed more for publicity than substance," both Bushmaster and the store settled out of court after mediation. In what the plaintiff's lawyers described as a "landmark" victory, Bushmaster Firearms agreed to pay $550,000, and Bull's Eye Shooter Supply of Tacoma agreed to pay $2 million.

The Brady Center to Prevent Gun Violence, which pressed the suit, crowed that the settlement "sends a loud message to all gun manufacturers." A Bushmaster lawyer begged to differ: "The Brady Center lawsuit was intended to put Bushmaster out of business or make it change its business practices," said attorney Steve Fogg. "Neither goal was accomplished." The company noted its insurance would pay the entire settlement.

Elapsed time from suit to settlement: about seventeen months.

Sources:

* "Families of 2 Sniper Victims File Suit," *Seattle Times*, 17 January 2003
* "Gun Dealer and Manufacturer Settle in Sniper Lawsuit," *Seattle Times*, 9 September 2004

```
1              *              )   Location: California
2         The State          )   Year: 2003
                             )
3            v.              )   Award Status:
4      Elderly Retired       )   Dishonorable Mention
                             )
5       Dry Cleaners         )
                             )
```

TAKING THEM TO
THE CLEANERS

Some people think the problem with outrageous lawsuits is so bad the government should step in. But sometimes the government is getting into the act itself.

The state of California has pulled out the big guns: It has sued a number of industrial polluters. The state says groundwater in the town of Chico is contaminated with perchloroethylene, otherwise known as perc or PCE, a common solvent used in dry cleaning since the 1930s.

In 1998 about 344 million pounds of PCE were used in the U.S. About 25 percent of that was used by the dry cleaning and textile processing sector; 50 percent was used in the manufacture of other chemicals, and the rest was used in other processes such as degreasing. Ironically, its use has actually increased in recent years since it's used in the manufacture of hydrofluorocarbons, the refrigerant used to replace chlorofluorocarbons in air-conditioning, because CFCs are thought to deplete the ozone layer.

Still, the state attorney general's office has filed suits against:

* Vart Vartabedian, age 93.

* Bob Heidinger, 87, and his wife, Inez, 83.

* Paul Tullius, 57, and his wife, Vicki.

* And many others, mostly elderly *former* dry cleaners. And also the city of Chico, because their sewers leak, causing decades-old PCE residues to seep into the ground.

"Whenever you're suing someone who is older or who ran a mom-and-pop dry cleaners, you do have sympathy for them," said Deputy Attorney General Rose Fua. On the other hand, she adds, "If somebody was 85 years old and they killed somebody, does the law not apply to them?"

Then how does the state explain the case against Tullius? The Air Force retiree bought a building in Chico in 1988 to house his old car collection. It's now leased to a homeless shelter. He had no idea when he bought the building that it housed a dry-cleaning business until 1972, and if he did it may not have occurred to him that it was something he needed to worry about. That doesn't matter to the state: They sued him anyway since he owns it *now*. The man he bought it from has "sort of become a friend, but I'm going to have to sue him" to protect himself, Tullius says. "And I suppose he'll have to sue the person he bought it from." He estimates it will cost him $75,000 to $100,000 in legal fees, not to mention countless hours of effort, to fight the state's suit.

"I fought in two wars," Tullius says. "I thought I've done everything right and now—can you imagine getting a bill like this for something we had absolutely nothing to do with? Can you imagine what that does to your life? I'm sort of thinking this isn't the country I thought it was."

Tullius aside, the others are indeed former dry cleaners. The state says they dumped PCE down the drain and caused the contamination. But the state doesn't seem to have any proof of its contentions. Bob Heidinger, for instance, says his machines never dumped PCE. In a sworn statement, he says his machines recycled the PCE, and that the residue was collected in buckets and dumped in the trash, which was standard procedure at the time.

"It's shocking that this should happen almost 30 years after we sold the business," Heidinger says. "I've worked all my life. We did nothing to cause this suit. Where is the proof? We never did anything wrong." He sold his business in 1974. The building it was in now houses a coffee shop.

How does the state respond? "We've identified who we think were the sources of the pollution," said a state spokesman. "We've done quite a bit of investigation up there." That makes the cases a matter of flimsy evidence versus the failing memories of long-retired small-business owners, which is hardly a good way to get to the truth.

But surely the dry cleaners had insurance. These days, insurance doesn't cover environmental cleanup, but thirty or forty years ago it usually did. Unfortunately, most of the defendants in the suits don't know where their decades-old insurance papers are. After ten or twenty years, they figured they didn't need to keep that sort of paperwork anymore. The state doesn't care.

"The groundwater in Chico is contaminated with PCE

and someone has to pay for cleaning this up," says Deputy Attorney General Fua—even though the state has already cleaned up Chico's groundwater and declared it safe to drink. "If we don't find the responsible parties, that means the taxpayers have to clean it up." So the state is going after a handful of people who likely don't have millions of dollars anyway, and can't defend themselves because they never imagined they'd need to take receipts and other documentation to court decades after they retired—papers they never dreamed it would be reasonable to need to have at their fingertips forever. "If they want to sue me, fine and dandy," Vartabedian says. "All I can do is go broke." He and a lot of other people who should be enjoying their retirement in peace.

The cases are still pending.

Sources:

* "State Is Suing Ex-Dry Cleaners," *Sacramento Bee*, 28 April 2003
* *White Paper: Perchloroethylene*, Halogenated Solvents Industry Alliance, November 1999

```
1              *            )  Location: Nevada
                            )
2        Grieving Mother    )  Year: 2004
                            )
3             v.            )  Award Status:
                            )  Dishonorable Mention
4      Anyone Within Sight  )
                            )
5  ------------------------- )
```

COORS SLIGHT

Ryan Pisco was at a party near the state university in Reno, drinking his favorite beer: Coors. By 2:45 A.M. he was drunk and left the party. Pisco, who did not have a driver's license, drove away in his girlfriend's car, which her mother had given to her.

He didn't make it home: Pisco hit a traffic light pole at ninety miles per hour and was killed.

Like many producers of alcoholic beverages, Coors not only discourages driving after drinking, it discourages alcohol use by underaged consumers. The legal drinking age in Nevada is 21. Pisco was just 19, but already had a "favorite beer."

Coors' public stand was not good enough for Ryan's mother, Jodie Pisco. Two years after the crash she sued Colorado-based Coors Brewing Company and its Reno distributor in Washoe District Court.

"Coors sponsors and supports events that are attractive to minors and youthful persons, glorifying a culture of youth, sex and glamour while hiding the dangers of alcohol abuse and addiction," the lawsuit charges. "Coors targets the youth of America with false images of conquest, achievement and success that are reckless, willful and a

deliberate disregard for the impact of illegal alcohol consumption by underage youths." The suit sought unspecified damages, said attorney Ken McKenna, who filed the
suit for Jodie Pisco.

"They should be well aware that people under 21 are
drinking Coors," McKenna told reporters. "They should be
liable for the damage caused by underage drinking."

If the suit stopped there, most people would have a little sympathy for it. But Pisco also sued her son's girlfriend, Heather Taylor, for allegedly allowing the adult lad
to drive off in her car. (Unfortunately, my sources don't address the obvious question of whether she was present or
not, or even whether she gave him permission to use her
car.) The suit also named the girl's mother, Janice Taylor,
since she gave the car to Heather.

It didn't stop there, either. Pisco also sued Joseph
Combs, the owner of the house where the party was held,
even though the suit didn't allege he was at the party, or
even knew about it. Also named in the suit was Jessica Ro-
driguez, who rented the house from Combs.

Coors didn't take the suit lying down: Nevada law prohibits lawsuits against alcoholic beverage manufacturers
in such cases. When Coors threatened McKenna with
sanctions for filing a frivolous suit, he dropped Coors
from the list of defendants.

Of course, McKenna used the move for publicity purposes, telling a reporter that "after doing some research,
we decided that the [Nevada] Supreme Court is unlikely to
be inclined politically to overturn the protection for alcohol distributors." McKenna went on to add that he wasn't
the one wanting all the publicity, but rather it was his
client, Jodie Pisco, who wanted the suit splashed across
the news to help show the dangers of underage drinking,

as if news reports of a lawsuit could somehow be more effective than a real story of a real teen being killed driving drunk—the stories about her own son.

Now, isn't that easy! Companies who can afford lawyers to defend against obviously frivolous suits can get out of them. Now only the grieving girlfriend, her innocent mother, the unknowing homeowner, and the girl renting the house are on the hook to defend against the mother's wrath. But that's known as "justice" in America.

Thankfully, McKenna wasn't so sure he wanted to go forward against that group, once Coors' deep pockets were out of the picture. Besides, he said, "The law does give some immunity even to people who serve alcohol." Oh, yeah, the law. Darn it how *that* gets in the way.

And don't forget Pisco's mother. If her son had been drinking beer long enough to have developed a taste for a "favorite," shouldn't she have known about his drinking and done something about it? If anyone is to blame for her son's actions—besides him, of course—why is his mother off the hook? If she couldn't control her son, why does she think anyone else could?

Coors' lawyers told McKenna that "it is simply wrong to exploit the Pisco family's grief by bringing baseless lawsuits against parties who are neither legally nor morally responsible for Ryan's death." I couldn't have said it better myself.

Sources:

* "Reno Mother's Lawsuit Targets Alcohol Providers," *Reno Gazette-Journal,* 16 April 2004
* "Lawyer Drops Suit Against Coors in Man's Death," *Reno Gazette-Journal,* 2 June 2004

1	*	) Location: California
2	Amateur Elephant Fan	) Year: 2003
3	v.	) Award Status:
4	Professional	) Dishonorable Mention
5	Elephant Keepers	)

NEW ZOO REVIEW

The Los Angeles Zoo announced plans to move Ruby, an African elephant, to the Knoxville, Tennessee, zoo so it could be with other African elephants and be a role model for other females on how to be a good mother. But Catherine Doyle, 46, filed a lawsuit in Los Angeles Superior Court asking for an order to prohibit the zoo from moving Ruby. She said that would separate her from Gita, an Asian elephant Ruby has lived with for sixteen years. (African and Asian elephants are different species of pachyderm.)

"We believe there is a special relationship between the two, and we think they should stay together the rest of their lives," said Doyle's attorney, Yael Trock, who specializes in personal injury litigation. Trock also said the elephants "should be kept in the city because we are the taxpayers and residents of the city and we should be the ones enjoying seeing them."

So on the one hand, the two elephants are special friends and it would be cruel to separate them, but on the other hand, they're taxpayer-purchased property that should benefit only the people who paid for them. In lawsuit circles it apparently makes perfectly good sense to argue out of both sides of your mouth.

Source:

* ⋆ "Suit Seeks to Keep Elephant at L.A. Zoo," *Los Angeles Times*, 15 May 2003

Afterword:

The L.A. Zoo did move Ruby, but she didn't fit in with the elephants in Knoxville. "Our goal was to incorporate her with a herd, not just send her to another location," said the zoo's general manager, John Lewis. "When that was not going to happen, we decided to bring her back." Catherine Doyle took credit for that, saying her lawsuit "pushed the zoo's hand."

In January 2005, Judge George H. Wu ruled that the suit could proceed but, because by then the elephant was back in Los Angeles, it could proceed only if the zoo attempted to move the elephant again in the foreseeable future. That was rendered moot when the city's mayor ordered the zoo to keep Ruby in town. Total elapsed court time: nearly two years.

Source:

* ⋆ "Ruby the Elephant Heading Back to L.A.," Associated Press, 20 July 2004
* ⋆ Court filings

Medical Cases
The Wrong Medicine

Doctors and other care providers sometimes make big mistakes and truly harm people. Such malpractice suits are a reasonable use of the courts. Other times, people view doctors and hospitals more as deep pockets full of money than as partners in responsible health care.

1	*	) Location: Pennsylvania
2	Unmotivated	) Year: 2002
3	v.	) Award Status: Runner-up
4	Everyone's Uncle	) for the 2002 Stella Award
5		)

NAH NAH NAH NAH
(I CAN'T HEAR YOU?)
NAH NAH NAH NAH

Every time you visit your doctor, you're told the same old things: Eat less, exercise more, stop smoking. Do you listen? Neither did Kathleen Ann McCormick. The obese, cigarette-smoking woman from Wilkes-Barre, Pennsylvania, had high blood pressure, high cholesterol, and a family history of coronary artery disease. Yet she said doctors at the Department of Veterans Affairs Medical Center "did not do enough" to convince her to work to improve her own health.

As any casual observer would not be surprised to hear, she had a heart attack which, she said in a lawsuit filed in the U.S. District Court for the Middle District of Pennsylvania, left her a "cardiac invalid." In addition to eight doctors, she sued their employer—the U.S. government—demanding a minimum of $1 million in compensation.

Exactly who doesn't know at this point that obesity is unhealthy? That cigarettes are killers? That high blood pressure dramatically increases the risk of strokes and heart attacks? The government spends millions of dollars getting the word out, but if you don't hold someone down and say, "We're talking to *you!*" they don't hear it. Whose problem is that, and who should pay when they refuse to listen? Hint: It ain't the taxpayers.

Source:

* "Woman Is Suing VA Doctors," *Wilkes-Barre Times-Leader,* 17 September 2002

```
1              *            ) Location: California
                            )
2       Several Sisters     ) Year: 2002
                            )
3             v.            ) Award Status: Winner of
                            ) the 2002 Stella Award
4   Their Mother's Doctors  )
                            )
5   ----------------------- )
```

NIED GIVEN DOSE OF
COMMON SENSE

In 1994, Nita Bird was brought to the hospital by her daughter, Janice, for a twenty-minute treatment for her ovarian cancer. After an hour, Janice asked what the delay was. About that time the doctor treating Nita called for assistance. About an hour later, Janice was told there was a complication.

Shortly after hearing that bad news, she saw her mother being rushed down the hall to critical care. Nita didn't look good: She was turning blue and swelling from internal bleeding. Then Janice's sister Dayle Edgmon arrived at the hospital, just in time for both sisters to see Nita again rushed down the hall, this time to emergency surgery, still looking extremely ill.

There may have been a legitimate claim for a malpractice case, since Nita's urgent condition was a result of her treatment, not her Stage IIIc cancer, but malpractice might have been pretty hard to prove. So Janice, Dayle, and a third sister, Kim Moran, sued for "negligent infliction of emotional distress," known as NIED in the lawsuit biz. Here's the odd twist: The NIED claim is not about the doctors causing distress to their mother. The suit claims the victims of the alleged negligent infliction of emotional distress are *the three sisters*, since having seen the doctors rush their stricken mother to surgery, "which allegedly saved Bird's life," was "traumatic" to *them*. To satisfy California's three-part test for NIED, the suit says they "were all present at the scene of the injury-producing events" and that "they were all aware that [the] Defendants, and each of them, were causing injury to their mother." The third part is being closely related to the victim.

The Los Angeles County Superior Court threw the suit out, granting summary judgment for the doctors on the basis that the sisters were not in the operating room when Nita's artery was accidentally nicked during the procedure, and therefore they were not "present at the scene of the injury-producing events." (Not to mention that the third sister, Moran, wasn't even in the state at the time of the procedure.)

The three sisters appealed, and a California appeals court reversed the Superior Court decision. Then the defense appealed, and the case ended up with the California Supreme Court which, eight years after the incident, unanimously ruled against the sisters and strengthened the three-part test for NIED.

And that is extremely important to every person in the state of California and, perhaps, the country. Why? If the sisters had prevailed and such a standard had been encoded in to case law, doctors and hospitals would have been forced to make family members stay away when they are treating people for fear of causing emotional distress in family members who see medical procedures, which (let's face it) can be bloody and painful. Forget that it is often beneficial to the patient to have a family member nearby; medical professionals simply wouldn't have been able to take the chance had the sisters established such a precedent.

Cheers to the common sense of the California Supreme Court, and a trio of Stella Awards to the Bird sisters for putting us all at the risk of not being allowed to be there for our own family members in their times of need.

Sources:

* "Women 'Distressed' by Seeing Doctors Rush to Help Mom," *American Medical News,* 2 September 2002
* "Janice Bird et al. v. Rolando Saenz et al.," California Supreme Court Opinion No. S095474, 12 August 2002

Is There a Malpractice Crisis?

The American Medical Association says twenty states* are in "crisis" due to a "deteriorating medical liability climate and the growing threat of patients' losing access to care." For instance, in Massachusetts, 50 percent of neurosurgeons, 41 percent of orthopedic surgeons, and 29 percent of general surgeons have said they have reduced their practices to avoid high-risk cases that tend to generate lawsuits. If all our doctors reject the worst cases, who will be left to treat us when we're seriously ill?

*Arkansas, Connecticut, Florida, Georgia, Illinois, Kentucky, Massachusetts, Mississippi, Missouri, New Jersey, Nevada, New York, North Carolina, Ohio, Oregon, Pennsylvania, Texas, Washington, West Virginia, and Wyoming. (*Source: American Medical Association*)

1	*	) Location: New Jersey
2	Teacher	) Year: 2003
3	v.	) Award Status:
4	Young Student	) Dishonorable Mention
5		)

HALLED INTO COURT

Daniel Allen, 11 years old and ninety pounds, was running to catch the school bus home when he ran into a teacher, Eileen Blau. He really did run into her: They collided in the hallway at E. T. Hamilton Elementary School in Voorhees, New Jersey.

The next day, Daniel was called to the principal's office and was told Blau was injured in the collision. He cried and apologized to the teacher.

All better, then? No. Two years later, Blau sued the boy in New Jersey Superior Court, claiming he "negligently and carelessly" ran into her at an "excessive rate of speed," which caused "severe and multiple injuries, some of which are permanent in nature." The suit says her injuries caused her to "curtail [her] normal activities."

Daniel's mother, Stacy Allen, said that when a sheriff's deputy served the lawsuit at her home, he was embarassed and "chagrined" to be serving papers on a 13-year-old.

"Maybe he should not have been running in the hall," she said, "but I think it was an accident. When you send a kid off to school, you expect him to be supervised and taken care of. You never expect a teacher to sue a child for running into her." Worse, she said, the boy was quite upset over being sued. "He didn't understand why someone would want to do this to him. He said 'Why does she hate me? Why is she doing this?' I said I was sorry."

Obviously, "sorry" doesn't always cut it, but when people are injured at work they're fully covered by workers' compensation insurance for their loss of wages and medical expenses due to their injuries. If the boy was truly out of control, whose fault was it? Maybe the people who were paid to instruct and supervise the child, such as Ms. Blau?

Source:

* "Teacher Sues Student over Hall Collision," *Cherry Hill Courier-Post*, 29 March 2003

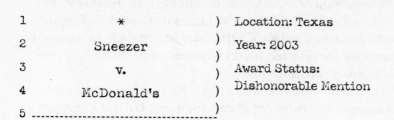

```
1              *              )  Location: Texas
                              )
2          Sneezer           )  Year: 2003
                              )
3            v.               )  Award Status:
                              )  Dishonorable Mention
4        McDonald's          )
                              )
5  -----------------------------)
```

A LAWSUIT THAT'S
NOTHING TO SNEEZE AT

Marcus Long, 61, has cancer in his brain, colon, lung, and spine—he's a very sick man. He and his wife Elaine moved to a new house in Clear Lake, Texas, to be close to medical care. "I was too scared to be more than twenty minutes from his doctors," Elaine said. They say he "nearly died" three times during 2002.

Marcus may be deathly ill, but like most people he likes to eat out once in a while, even though he obviously needs to be careful. He favors McDonald's, where nearly every morning Elaine got him three sausage, egg, and cheese breakfast burritos, plus two pints of milk to wash them down—he needed something soft because radiation treatments and chemotherapy made his mouth so sore, he couldn't wear his dentures.

But one day, the burritos she brought home were "filled" with pepper, and when Marcus bit into one he choked and got a nosebleed. She took the burritos back to McDonald's but found the manager "wasn't apologetic or anything." Worse, the manager didn't offer a refund or a free Happy Meal.

Elaine said Marcus went "downhill" after the event, and has nosebleeds regularly. The Longs thus sued McDonald's in Galveston County Court, alleging breach of implied warranty for offering food as "wholesome" that was "unfit for human consumption."

Dr. Leslie Botnick, a Los Angeles radiation oncologist, was asked to comment about the case. He did not examine Mr. Long, but he's quite familiar with how pepper consumption irritates cancer patients' systems.

Botnick called the pepper exposure "a onetime event." Clearly it can be irritating, but Marcus "spit it out. It's not gonna be there on a daily basis. If you buy a burrito, it's sometimes gonna be hot. That's what burritos do."

Botnick added that cancer patients often bleed—but it's usually due to their cancers, not from eating pepper, Dr. Botnick said, adding, "Pepper does not promote cancer."

If McDonald's put a lot of pepper into a food item that normally doesn't have added pepper, shame on them. The manager was out of line if she didn't apologize or refund the Longses' money. It's sad for anyone to have to suffer an early and painful death, but should it be McDonald's responsibility to ensure their food is acceptable for every person with every possible condition, even a man on his deathbed? The Longs may be angry to be "victims," but they're victims of life, not McDonald's. Still, corporations need to learn how to say "sorry"—as long as lawyers and courts don't pounce on a decent human apology as evidence of liability.

Source:

* "Mac Attack—a Cancer Patient Sues McDonald's, Contending a Peppered Burrito Caused His Nosebleed," *Houston Press*, 16 January 2003

```
1                *              ) Location: Missouri
                                )
2         Bad Hair Day          ) Year: 2003
                                )
3              v.               ) Award Status:
                                ) Dishonorable Mention
4         Hair Salon            )
                                )
5 -----------------------------)
```

HAIR TODAY, GONE
TOMORROW

Geremie Hoff, 55, went to the Elizabeth Arden Salon at the Saks Fifth Avenue store in St. Louis to get her hair straightened in August 2001. She said that later, on a trip, some of her hair fell out and her scalp was "flaky." Some weeks after that, "her hair stuck out like a bird's nest," said her attorney, Paul Devine.

That caused Hoff to "shut down," Devine says. "She spiraled into a depression because, right or wrong, looks were important to her." Because of that alleged depression, Hoff said, she took early retirement from her teaching job at the University of Missouri at St. Louis and quit her side job of taking tour groups to Italy.

The salon's lawyer noted Hoff left a tip after her hair treatment, indicating she was satisfied at the time. Her "alleged losses were unrelated to anything we did," said attorney Lawrence Hartstein. And any hair that had fallen out had regrown before her next scheduled trip to Italy, and she didn't retire from the university until a year after her visit to the salon. Also, he noted that Hoff admitted she sometimes colored her hair herself, and that may have contributed to any problems she may have had with her hair.

Still, Hoff sued the salon, not specifying a specific amount that would compensate her for her "emotional distress." Her attorney, however, said her lost income alone was worth $45,000.

A St. Louis County jury decided that the hairstylist should have tested the straightening solution on a strand of Hoff's hair before applying it to the rest of the hair on her head. On that basis it awarded her $6,000. The salon was responsible for the whole amount, since the lawsuit didn't name the hairstylist. Not exactly a bad hair day, even though it took Hoff nearly two years to get her verdict.

Sources:

* "Hair-Uncurling Experience Prompts Suit," *St. Louis Post-Dispatch,* 8 April 2003
* "Jury Awards Creve Coeur Woman $6,000 in Suit over Hairdo," *St. Louis Post-Dispatch,* 9 April 2003

```
1              *              )   Location: Washington
2       Grave Stepper        )   Year: 2003
                             )
3            v.              )   Award Status:
                             )   Dishonorable Mention
4        Graveyard           )
                             )
5   --------------------------)
```

DEAD TO RIGHTS

Dorothy VerValen, 51, visited her grandfather's fifty-three-year-old grave in Sultan, Washington. There was some moss on his headstone, so she stepped on the grave to scrape it off.

When she stepped on the grave, VerValen, who weighed 375 pounds, collapsed the dirt and her right foot sank into the ground. Her left foot stayed on firm ground, and her left ankle was broken.

"I literally had one foot in the grave," she said. "I thought I was in a Stephen King movie."

No, she wasn't in a horror movie, but rather a courtroom drama—she sued the city claiming it was negligent, seeking unspecified damages for injuries, emotional distress, and legal costs.

"The city of Sultan wants people to walk around, but they don't need to be out there every minute making it safe," said the city's lawyer, Diana Blakney.

"They know sinkholes happen, especially in pre-1960s graves," said VerValen's lawyer, Robert Butler, but "they're not doing anything to prevent it from happening." Older graves are subject to sinkholes when the coffin rots away, leaving an open space six feet below the surface. But the only sinkholes that have appeared in the Sultan Cemetery were the result of "heavy equipment" breaking through, Blakney said. Newer burial vaults are generally lined with concrete, which reduces the chance of such problems.

Blakney argued the state's Recreational Use Act applied to the cemetery. That law notes that users of recreational facilities are responsible for their own safety. The cemetery is open twenty-four hours a day and does not charge any admission.

If someone must be held responsible for VerValen's injuries, why not her own family, who buried Grampa in a coffin that could rot away when they could have used a concrete-lined vault? Or, more realistically, how about if she took responsibility for herself, when she "knows or should have known" that not every hollow structure can support someone who tilts the scale at a fifth of a ton?

Snohomish County Superior Court Judge Richard Thorpe dismissed the lawsuit. He ruled, according to the plaintiff's attorney, "that the weight of Mrs. VerValen is the substantial factor" behind her injury. VerValen complained that "everybody says it's because of my weight, but my 2-year-old grandson could have fallen in there"— completely missing the irony in her own statement, since a 2-year-old certainly wouldn't have punched through the ground. Unless, of course, he weighed a fifth of a ton.

At least it's nice to know that cases can still be decided on the weight of the evidence. Total time from injury to case dismissal: twenty-seven months.

Sources:

* "Grave Encounter at Sinkhole Leads to Suit," *Portland Oregonian,* 29 May 2003

✳ "Judge Waives Suit in Mishap at Sultan Grave," *Seattle Times,* June 18, 2003

⚖ Obstetrics Crisis

Pregnant women may be the biggest victims of overzealous medical lawsuits. The American College of Obstetricians and Gynecologists reports that as of 2004, twenty-three states* are in "red alert" crisis status, up from sixteen in 2002. "Women's health care is at a very critical point. Without relief, women will be desperate to find prenatal and gynecologic care, and many pregnant women will scramble to find doctors to deliver their babies," says ACOG president Vivian M. Dickerson, MD. "It's truly alarming that this access-to-health-care crisis has become so profound and widespread."

*In "full-blown crisis": District of Columbia, Florida, Georgia, Nevada, New Jersey, New York, Ohio, Oregon, Pennsylvania, Virginia, Washington, and Wyoming. Crisis is "brewing": Alabama, Arizona, Connecticut, Illinois, Kentucky, Maryland, Missouri, and Utah. Being "monitored" are Mississippi, Texas, and West Virginia. (*Source: ACOG*)

```
1              *              )   Location: New York
                             )
2        An Unhandy Man      )   Year: 2003
                             )
3             v.             )   Award Status:
                             )   Dishonorable Mention
4        Restroom Door       )
                             )
5  ---------------------------)
```

HEADS UP—WAY UP

Cedrick Makara, 55, went to the restroom at the building where he worked in New York City. The door to his loo didn't have a knob, just a hole where the knob should have been. He stuck his hand through the hole to open it just as someone else came in, hitting the door. Makara, a city employee, jammed his hand.

The injury was no laughing matter: He had to have surgery to fix tendons in his thumb. But six months off work (remember, he's a government employee) and medical care wasn't anywhere near enough: He sued the building's private owner and manager for failing to fix the door.

The result: Makara was awarded $2 million for past and future pain and suffering, $200,000 for future medical needs, and $750,000 for his wife. Yep, he hit the jackpotty: almost $3 million when he used a facility where he knew the doorknob was missing before he was injured.

In a delicious twist, Makara's job with the city: claims examiner. Doesn't that make him one of the guys who watches out for people trying to extort money from the city with frivolous claims?

Total time from incident to multimillionaire: about four years.

Source:

*   "He's Flush after $3m Potty Suit," *New York Daily News*, 21 May 2003

```
1                    *          )   Location: Alabama
                                )
2        The Self-Stored        )   Year: 2003
                                )
3              v.               )   Award Status: Runner-up
                                )   for the 2003 Stella Award
4        Storage Facility       )
                                )
5
```

THE COUNTESS OF
MONTE CRISTO

Wanda Hudson of Mobile, Alabama, lost her home to foreclosure. Her lawyer, Mallory Mantiply, said the creditor tossed her possessions "into the street." Hudson, who was 42 at the time, rented one of the 456 units at Parkway Storage, just two miles from her house, to store her belongings.

A month later, on November 7, 2001, Hudson paid for another month's rent on her three-hundred-square-foot storage unit. Later that night she was inside. In making his rounds, Parkway Storage's manager noticed the door was unlocked and slightly open. He locked it up and moved on. Hudson was still inside.

Certainly anyone locked into such a place would yell and scream, pound on the door, and demand to be let out. But Hudson didn't do that. Incredibly, she made virtually no attempt to let anyone know she was trapped. She subsisted on juice and canned foods that she had stored in the unit.

Parkway Storage's attorney Bert Taylor said another storage customer whose unit was two spaces away went to her own storage space almost "every single day," yet never heard a thing. "There was no yelling, no screaming, no beating on the doors, no nothing," he said. "No one knew she was in there." And she was there for a long, long time.

It wasn't until January 9, 2002, sixty-three days after she was locked inside, when someone heard noises—not yelling or banging, just "noises"—from inside the locked unit and notified the storage company. The door was opened and Hudson, who had been a "plump" 150 pounds, was in horrific condition: She weighed only eighty-five pounds and her doctor said she was in "advanced starvation, unusual to find in medical circumstances in America today." Her fingernails, normally several inches long, were said to be a foot in length. The smell inside was so bad that fire department rescue personnel donned gas masks before going in. Hudson was so disoriented she hadn't realized she had missed Thanksgiving and Christmas.

Sad indeed, but someone must be held responsible, right? Well, someone other than her, anyway: Hudson and her lawyer claimed Parkway Storage was solely responsible for her plight and sued the company for $10 million in Mobile County Circuit Court, claiming negligence.

During the trial, Hudson was "vague" in her testimony about why she was in the unit late at night, and why she didn't hear the manager lock the door. She denied she was asleep, and denied she was living in the unit. She claimed she was "looking for some papers" and just didn't hear the door shut and lock behind her. She said, "I screamed, I banged, I banged, I banged," whenever she heard anyone nearby. But, she said, everyone ignored her cries for help.

When Hudson testified she was not living in her storage unit, but rather lived with her sister, defense attorney Taylor asked her, "Was she expecting you that night?"

Yes, Hudson said. Yet her sister was not concerned with Hudson's absence of over two months—she never filed a missing person report.

Just a week before being trapped in her storage unit, Hudson was assessed by mental health authorities. They declared she posed "a real and present threat of substantial harm to herself and/or others." They described Hudson as unable to "physically take care of herself . . . allowing her physical condition to deteriorate to the point of threatening her health and well-being, making threats to kill herself." Yet when it came to her lawsuit against the storage company, Circuit Judge Rick Stout ruled that evidence inadmissible; the defense couldn't bring it up.

After a two-day trial, the jury was briefly deadlocked at eight to four—but it was not revealed in whose favor. The judge "reminded the jury of their duty," and two hours later they decided in Hudson's favor and awarded her $100,000. The jury, however, was clearly bothered by Hudson not doing more to free herself: In addition to awarding her only one percent of the suit's begged-for amount, they asked the judge questions about a person's "own responsibility for his or her predicament" before they made their decision.

Surely Hudson's mental situation provides an understandable—if rather bizarre—explanation for why she didn't try to get help for over two months once she realized she was locked in her unit. Yet the jury wasn't allowed to learn of that important detail, and felt sorry enough for her to award her substantial damages. Hudson was destitute enough that she lost her home, but was able to become wealthy by making someone else pay for her own negligence brought on by her mental problems. In a court of law, that's known as justice. In the Court of Public Opinion, it's known as something else entirely: a Stella Award.

Total elapsed time for the case: almost twenty months, not counting the time Hudson was in storage.

Sources:

* "Woman Sues DIP Storage Facility over Bizarre Ordeal," *Mobile Register,* 26 September 2003
* "Woman Seeks $10 Million in Storage Facility Ordeal," *Mobile Register,* 27 September 2003
* "Locked-up Woman Awarded $100,000," *Mobile Register,* 30 September 2003

Afterword:

"Got to disagree with your conclusions on this one," a reader said. "Wanda did not lock herself into her storage unit; the unit manager did it. His action, his responsibility. His negligence, too. It amazes me that he didn't check into the unit before locking it—I would have thought that would be basic training. Wanda's mental incompetence could well have contributed to the length of time she was in there, but who can tell for sure? The amount actually awarded seems reasonable to me."

The issue here isn't the action—locking her in. Would $100,000 be reasonable if he locked the door and, while he was walking away, Hudson yelled, *"Hey! Open that door!"* and he went right back and let her out? If so, then maybe the reader is right. However, the damage wasn't caused by being locked in, but by being locked in for sixty-three days. And this was *solely* due to Hudson's mental illness because she quite simply did not call out for help—for two months! The crux of the Stella Award was that the jury was *prohibited* from hearing evidence about her mental illness, which quite clearly explains why she didn't call out. Indeed, even though the jury didn't have that key bit of information, it still only awarded her one percent of her asked-for damages.

1	*	)	Location: Illinois
2	Stella, Jr.	)	Year: 2004
3	v.	)	Award Status:
4	Another Burger Joint	)	Dishonorable Mention
5		)	

HIS LAWYER CAN RUN RINGS AROUND YOURS

Michael Strauss of Chicago was tucking into a burger and onion rings from a White Castle restaurant in Bourbonnais, Illinois, when, upon biting into one of the onion rings, "scalding hot grease splattered out and onto" his arm, "scalding and severely burning him." Two years later he sued the burger chain for the "severe and permanent injuries" he says he suffered from the "unreasonably dangerous" food.

Onion rings, of course, are cooked by submerging them into hot grease. So how does he justify that they were "unreasonably dangerous"? The court filing says they were served in "defective condition" (which apparently means "freshly dumped from the fryer basket"), which left him in "great pain and anguish in mind and body." The suit, filed with the help of attorney Janine Rosana, demands $50,000 in compensation.

The *Chicago Sun-Times* found the case reminiscent of

the original Stella Liebeck case against McDonald's. The case is apparently still pending.

Source:

* "White Castle Lawsuit Has Familiar Ring," *Chicago Sun-Times,* 30 September 2004

```
1              *           )   Location: California
                           )
2         Lawyer's Wife    )   Year: 2003
                           )
3              v.          )   Award Status:
                           )   Dishonorable Mention
4           Darwin         )
                           )
5   --------------------------)
```

"HINDSIGHT, OF COURSE, IS A MARVELOUS THING"

John Kincannon, 46, was a successful attorney. He practiced real estate law in Irvine, California, and was a "prominent litigator," said the Kincannon's family attorney, Wylie A. Aitken.

Kincannon lived in a nice Orange County house with the requisite swimming pool. He was not above cleaning it himself, either. One day he was skimming debris from his pool with a net on a long metal pole when he noticed that a palm frond was hanging from a power line in the yard. Apparently wanting to keep everything tidy, he decided to pull the frond down with the tool he had at hand—the metal pole.

Not surprisingly, Kincannon was electrocuted.

"Hindsight, of course, is a marvelous thing," attorney Aitken said, with no sense of irony. He noted the victim "was only being a good citizen in trying to get rid of this palm frond," as if it were bothering anyone but Kincannon.

Naturally, like most electric utilities, Southern California Edison runs what they call an "aggressive" ongoing publicity campaign to tell people not to try to get things out of power lines by themselves, urging them to call the company for help instead.

"It's tragic what happened to Mr. Kincannon," said SCE spokesman Tom Boyd. But, he added, considering the company has worked hard to keep people from getting anywhere near the power lines, "we're a little surprised that we might be served with a lawsuit."

Yes, a lawsuit. Kincannon's widow, Francilene, sued Edison in Orange County Superior Court. The suit also names Leslie's Swimming Pool Supplies, because the skimmer pole didn't have a warning label on it to tell people that it's not smart to stick metal poles into overhead power lines. "There's a great deal of information not available to homeowners like Kincannon," Aitken claims, hoping someone would actually believe that the power company is trying to keep commonsense safety rules secret.

Edison has devoted more than reasonable resources to warn its customers about dangers that should be obvious to all, let alone a highly educated person. And what silliness for the widow's suit to claim yet another warning label in an already overcrowded sea of caution notices would have helped when common sense didn't. There's only one other person who could possibly be to blame here, but Charles Darwin is exempt from court actions.

The case is still pending.

Source:

* "Death Suit Names Utility," *Los Angeles Times*, 19 August 2003

It's Not My Responsibility
Someone Else Needs to Pay

In America's growing culture of victimization, there is no such thing as an accident. In fact, there's no such thing as personal responsibility. If you're not to blame for something bad that happens to you, the thinking goes, then surely someone *else* is to blame. And if someone else can be found to take the blame, shouldn't they be made to pay? In America, a lawsuit is at the top of that house of cards.

```
1                    *              )   Location: New York
2          Heavy Eater            )   Year: 2003
                                   )
3              v.                  )   Award Status: Runner-up
4   The Fast-Food Industry  )       for the 2003 Stella Award
                                   )
5   -----------------------------------  )
```

AND THE McBANDWAGON
PLAYS ON

Caesar Barber, 56, of New York City, is five-foot-ten and weighs 270 pounds. He says he is obese as a result of eating burgers, chicken, and other fast food from various national restaurant chains four to five times per week. He continued chowing down the high-fat fare even after he had a heart attack. Then he had a second, and is a diabetic, and still didn't put two and two together. Why?

"They never explained to me what I was eating," Barber complained, ignoring the irony of not looking at what he stuffed into his mouth. For years, fast-food companies have had nutritional information, including fat content, available to consumers who ask. Those too embarrassed to ask can check the companies' Web sites. Apparently, Barber never bothered to do any of that. Should the restaurants be liable for his failure to utilize those resources to learn what he was eating?

Absolutely, said Barber's lawyer, Samuel Hirsch. "It's a question of informing the consumers." The restaurants, which "profited enormously," Hirsch said, have an "obligation" to warn their customers that eating their food can be "dangerous." Apparently their counter clerks were supposed to hold Barber down while he read the pamphlets tucked into the information bin on the wall, turning the pages for him and administering a quiz at the end.

The resulting lawsuit argues that Barber is obese, suffered heart attacks, and got diabetes not because of any action he is responsible for, but rather because of the dastardly, underhanded, profit-seeking actions of McDonald's, Burger King, Wendy's, and KFC. The lawsuit against the restaurant chains was filed in the New York State Supreme Court seeking unspecified damages (read: "money to go— and Super Size it, please!"). The suit was filed not just for himself, but—thanks to class-action status—for any and all other New Yorkers who were obese and suffering health problems after pounding down fast food. Fast food that they stopped to get, that they ordered, that they paid for, and that they ate, all without being at gunpoint.

The suit claims that the restaurants did not "properly disclose" their food ingredients nor the "risks" of eating junk food day after day after day. They sold their high-fat, high-sodium, high-sugar, high-cholesterol menu items even though studies show a link between overeating such food and obesity, coronary artery disease, hypertension, strokes, cancer, and diabetes—studies that have not been kept secret from the public at large. Yet Barber was shocked (*shocked!*) to discover that it wasn't healthy to eat such food in the quantities he consumed after suffering two heart attacks and the onset of diabetes.

"To win his suit he has to convince a jury or a judge that people are too stupid to feed themselves or their children," said John Doyle of the Center for Consumer Freedom, a restaurant trade group. "If people are so stupid, should they be allowed to vote or go to work in the morning?"

And if Barber did win, would Americans be allowed to choose what to have for lunch, or would they have to sign a release before ordering?

Surely the lawsuit can't be serious. Or can it? Barber's lawsuit "has a great deal of potential," said Professor John Banzhaf III of the George Washington University Law School after it was filed, even though "we know from the tobacco litigation that initial suits have real difficulties because the public has real problems accepting new ideas and new concepts." But by filing lawsuit after lawsuit, trying one novel legal theory after another, the lawyers finally won: Juries eventually came around and the tobacco companies had to pay. Banzhaf said he would act as an adviser to Barber. Perhaps he would argue that adding salt was similar to the tobacco companies adding nicotine to help addict smokers.

Barber's case drew others in, despite it already getting class-action status. A similar suit was filed in federal court by a group that included a four-hundred-pound 15-year-old boy who ate at McDonald's every day. It didn't take long for that case to be thrown out. U.S. District Court Judge Robert Sweet ruled that "legal consequences should not attach to the consumption of hamburgers and other fast-food fare unless consumers are unaware of the dangers of eating such food."

Which, of course, leaves the question open. The suit can be filed again if it is amended to address the judge's objections. How likely is that to happen?

"They are a talented and determined group of attorneys not to be underestimated," said New York attorney Thomas Bezanson, who proclaimed himself "delighted" at Judge Sweet's ruling "because it is so utterly correct." So will there be more such McCases? "You can be sure of it," he said. Forget the restaurants: Every American should take that as a threat.

Sources:

* "Whopper of a Lawsuit—Fast-Food Chains Blamed for Obesity, Illnesses," ABCnews.com, 26 July 2002
* "Obesity Suit Against McDonald's Dismissed," Reuters, 22 January 2003
* "Let Them Eat Cake," *Health Law Perspectives* (publication of the University of Houston Health Law & Policy Institute), 30 August 2002

Afterword:

"So will there be more such McCases?" I asked in the conclusion of the case. "You can be sure of it," said an observer. Sure enough, attorney Samuel Hirsch, who filed the case, as well as the other representing obese teens, has won a round. The Second U.S. Circuit Court of Appeals in New York has reversed the dismissal of the suit filed on behalf of the two teens. Judge Jed Rakoff reinstated the case, saying it should at least go to the discovery stage. Attorney Hirsch promises to look into "the ingredients, the advertisements, the type of representations that [McDonald's] made" to lure those poor, poor kids into thinking McDonald's food items "were healthy and wholesome, not as detrimental to their health as medical and scientific studies have shown."

Meanwhile, a legislator in New Mexico has introduced a bill officially titled the "Right to Eat Enchiladas Act," which is designed "to prevent frivolous lawsuits against manufacturers, packers, distributors, carriers, holders, sellers, marketers or advertisers of food . . . for any claim of injury arising out of weight gain, obesity, a health condition associated with weight gain or obesity or other generally known condition allegedly caused by or likely to result from the long-term consumption of food." About fourteen states have already passed similar laws, many in direct response to the current assault against McDonald's and other fast-food restaurants.

Sources:

* "Fast-Food Suit Back on the Menu: Appeals Court Reinstates Class Action Against McDonald's," *ABA Journal,* 28 January 04
* "Right to Eat Enchiladas Act," State of New Mexico Senate Bill 291, 2005

1	*	)	Location: West Virginia
2	Grieving Mother	)	Year: 2002
3	v.	)	Award Status:
4	Everyone She Can	)	Dishonorable Mention
5	Think Of	)	

HERE'S TO YOU . . . BEING RESPONSIBLE FOR ME

Dustin W. Bailey, 22, spent the evening of August 12, 2000, drinking in a bar in Teays Valley, West Virginia. Apparently seeking a warm place to lie down after he left the bar, he crawled under a truck sitting in front of a pizza parlor across the street.

The truck's driver was inside the restaurant making a delivery. When he came out, he got in his truck and drove away. He had no idea anyone was under the truck; Bailey was run over and killed. A postmortem found he had a blood-alcohol level of 0.19 percent, nearly double the 0.10 percent legal presumption of intoxication in that state.

A tragic accident? Well, no, said Bailey's mother, Josephine Bailey of Hometown, West Virginia. She said her son certainly wouldn't have crawled under a truck voluntarily. "We just can't imagine our son doing that," she said at the time. (So we're to assume she had never seen him—or anyone else—drunk?) Since he just wouldn't do such a thing, *someone else* must take the blame for her son's death.

So she filed a lawsuit in Putnam County Circuit Court asking for more than $350,000 from:

* Papa John's Pizza, because its Teays Valley restaurant "forced" the truck driver to park on a public street—right in the way of her staggering son.

* The truck driver, Samuel T. Stinson. The suit says Stinson should have looked under his truck before driving away, and he should have shut off the engine when he left it on the street.

* The truck's owner, Rollins Transportation Systems, Inc.

* Rick's Pub, where Bailey had been drinking, and its owner, Richard E. Parsons, since the bar should have stopped serving him when he became intoxicated. (Wasn't that why Bailey left?)

Traffic fatalities are investigated by the police. What did the Putnam County Sheriff's Department have to say about who might be responsible for Bailey's death? "If anyone should be blamed for that death," said Chief Deputy John Dailey, "it's that guy who climbed under the truck"—Bailey himself. Dailey found it "surprising" that his mother would sue over his self-inflicted death.

Imagine the anguish truck driver Samuel Stinson felt when he discovered he had accidentally killed someone he didn't even know was there. Who looks under their cars before they drive away? He found out what happened when two men came running up to him. "Two guys yelled at me and told me that he was terrible drunk and that he had climbed under my trailer," he told police after the accident.

No doubt if Mrs. Bailey finds out who those two guys are she'll sue them, too, since surely everyone anywhere near her drunken, adult son that night had a duty to safeguard him. Everyone but himself, of course—his responsibility had been dissolved away in alcohol.

Source:

* "Woman Files Suit Over Son's Death," *Charleston Daily Mail*, 10 August 2002

1	*	)	Location: Rhode Island
2	Nightclub Victims	)	Year: 2003
3	v.	)	Award Status:
4	Everyone in the World	)	Dishonorable Mention
5		)	

SMOKE GETS IN
YOUR EYES

The tragic February 2003 fire at the Station Night-club in West Warwick, Rhode Island, killed nearly one hundred people and injured many more. Early indications were that the Station's owner used cheap foam to provide soundproofing around the stage—very flammable foam that quickly spread the fire, when more expensive noncombustible foam should have been used. And featured band Great White, which set off fireworks inside the packed club during its performance, is also alleged to be very much at fault.

Naturally, even before the smoke cleared, the smell of lawsuits filled the air. With so many dead, legal observers expect settlements and judgments will reach $1 billion. Surely the burned-out nightclub and band won't have that much in assets or insurance coverage. Who, then, would have that kind of money? If the lawyers could figure out who had money and had any involvement whatever with the event, they would then know whom to sue. Anyone. Anyone at all.

Radio station WHJY-FM in Providence ran advertisements for the concert, and Michael Gonsalves, a WHJY disk jockey, was there to introduce the band. (Gonsalves, by the way, is one of the dead.) WHJY is owned by Clear Channel Communications, which owns more than twelve hundred radio and TV stations, as well as other media properties.

A gigantic media corporation, you say? And one of its outlets helped lure poor, innocent victims ... er, *customers*! ... to the show? Good enough, say two Providence lawyers: They announced they would name Clear Channel in the suits they were filing to get their share of that billion-dollar damage estimate.

Attorney Steven Minicucci, the president of the Rhode Island Trial Lawyers Association, represents two people injured in the fire as well as the family of one man who died. He says Clear Channel "bears considerable responsibility" for the fatalities and injuries because the commercials it ran for the show did so well that the nightclub was overcrowded. "Their hands are all over this event," he says.

Attorney Max Wistow, who represents a number of victims, claims that ethical considerations *demand* that he name Clear Channel. "Any lawyer who didn't exhaustively explore their relationship to this thing and the facts surrounding their participation would be absolutely remiss and guilty of legal malpractice," he argues, as if that doesn't show, in and of itself, that there's something very, very wrong with America's civil court system.

What was WHJY's official involvement in the concert? Station general manager Bud Paras says the station was not a sponsor, but merely produced and ran fifteen thirty-second commercials for the event, for which it was paid $700. The station was also given, and gave away, just four tickets to the concert.

Rhode Island attorney Edward C. Roy, who doesn't represent any victims, finds the whole idea of involving Clear Channel a bit far-fetched. "I don't think it's necessarily a clear case of liability," he says, "but given the huge economic loss suffered by the victims, you'll definitely see them named. Of the people who are involved, they're probably the most well insured. They've got the deepest pockets." Those, to be sure, are sweet words to a litigator. Well, the last two sentences, anyway.

But why bring in Clear Channel at all? In many states, including Rhode Island, the system is designed to "help make injured parties whole" using the legal doctrine known as "joint and several liability." What that means is the entire judgment can be collected from *any* at-fault defendant, so if another defendant goes bankrupt (such as the nightclub in this case), the plaintiffs can still collect their reward. Thus, even if Clear Channel is judged to be only one-tenth of 1 percent at fault, they could be forced to pay as much as 100 percent of any awards which, again, are estimated to total in the vicinity of $1 billion for all the cases. So if the lawyers in the case can paint a horrible enough picture of the hundred dead bodies and get the jury to agree that the Big Bad Rich Corporation (er . . . Clear Channel)—or any other well-heeled defendant—bears just a minuscule amount of responsibility, the plaintiffs will win the jackpot: Clear Channel will have to cover any part of the billion or so bucks that any other defendant can't pay.

With that logic, *anyone* who promoted the concert is as much as 100 percent liable—such as people who heard about the concert and told a friend. Is that reasonable? Is that fair? Why should any person or company be made to pay any portion of the blame assigned to someone else? Joint and several liability is all about "helping make injured parties whole." Unfortunately, the doctrine doesn't take into account how it can destroy anyone who happens to be in its path, when the damage done to the people who were in the wrong place at the wrong time is merrily transferred to those who weren't.

Source:

* "R.I. Fire Victims' Lawyers Eye Firm; Suits Expected to Name Radio Station's Owner," *Boston Globe*, 8 March 2003

Afterword:

Over time the list of defendants in the case expanded to more than forty-five as other deep pockets were identified. In addition to the nightclub owners, the list includes the state fire marshal, for failing to personally be there to ensure there were not too many people inside; CBS television, because a local station's cameraman was inside and maybe, just perhaps, he got in the way of people trying to run after the fire started; the city fire inspector, for failing to note that flammable foam was used on the stage for soundproofing; the company that made the foam, even though it was not sold as fireproof material; the nightclub's insurance company, because it didn't discover that the soundproofing foam wasn't fireproof; Anheuser-Busch, who makes Budweiser beer, which was served at the nightclub; and, naturally, the band Great White, for allegedly starting the fire—probably one of the few defendants that makes sense in the case. But they don't have hundreds of millions of dollars in assets or insurance to pay the claims, so that's why everyone else is named. Because without deep pockets, the plaintiffs can't cash in.

Joint and Several Liability

"Joint and several liability" is considered so unfair that thirty-seven states* have enacted some form of joint and several liability reform legislation, either modifying it partially or completely abolishing the practice.

*Alaska, Arkansas, Arizona, California, Colorado, Connecticut, Florida, Georgia, Hawaii, Idaho, Illinois, Iowa, Kentucky, Louisiana, Michigan, Minnesota, Mississippi, Missouri, Montana, Nebraska, Nevada, New Hampshire, New Jersey, New Mexico, New York, North Dakota, Ohio, Oregon, Pennsylvania, South Dakota, Texas, Utah, Vermont, Washington, West Virginia, Wisconsin, Wyoming.

(*Source: National Association of Mutual Insurance Companies*)

```
1              *            )  Location: Minnesota
                            )
2        Big Game Hunter    )  Year: 2003
                            )
3             v.            )  Award Status:
                            )  Dishonorable Mention
4        Bullet Manufacturer)
                            )
5  -------------------------)
```

BIG SHOT

Rolf Rohwer of Scotland is a "professional" big game hunter, and went on a safari in Africa to shoot game. When a lion charged him, he shot it—but the lion managed to keep going, crossing thirty yards to maul him.

The problem, Rohwer said, was he was trying out a new type of ammunition in his hunting rifle, and it wasn't the right sort of ammunition to blow away a charging lion. But a "professional" knows his tools, and a sportsman knows there's risk, so that's the end of it, right?

Not by a long shot.

"This bullet is not suitable for killing a charging lion," said his American attorney, Louis Franecke of San Rafael, California. "It's suitable for killing a lion over a period of time." Except safari hunters aren't there to kill animals "over a period of time," they want those animals dead instantly. "The lion died basically while chewing on my client," Franecke says.

So on Rohwer's behalf, Franecke filed a U.S. federal lawsuit against Federal Cartridge Company of Anoka, Minnesota. The bullet Rohwer used is designed for thick-skinned big game, such as rhinos and hippos; the lion has thinner skin, which allowed the bullet to pass through its body without causing it to expand, making it less lethal, Franecke says. Thus, the shot lion remained a "harmful beast capable of causing severe personal injuries to humans for a substantial period of time," the lawsuit says. Yeah, well, who loaded the bullet into the rifle?

How much compensation Rohwer demanded was not reported. Who is responsible when a "professional" hunter uses the wrong ammunition for the job? Rohwer seemed to feel that in the safari world, turnabout is anything but fair play.

Source:

* "Injured Big-game Hunter Takes Aim at Bullet Manufac-turers," *Minneapolis Star Tribune,* 16 April 2003

Afterword:

Rohwer's lawsuit against Federal Cartridge Company charged defective design and "failure to warn" over that defect. But U.S. District Court Chief Judge James M. Rosenbaum threw the case out, calling the hunter's arguments "sheer conjecture." He also ruled that Rohwer failed to demonstrate that the bullet was dangerous (now, there's an interesting concept!), or that the manufacturer had any duty to warn him about its appropriateness for shooting lions. He also dismissed claims for breach of warranty, negligence, and design defect.

Total elapsed time from incident to conclusion of the lawsuit: four years, three months.

Source:

* "Big Game Hunter Fails to Bag Expert Testimony of Defect, Causation," *Product Safety & Liability Reporter,* 20 December 2004

1		*	)	Location: Alabama
2		Grieving Mother	)	Year: 2003
3		v.	)	Award Status:
4		Innocent Driver	)	Dishonorable Mention
5			)	

WHAT COMES AROUND, GOES AROUND

Charles McCall, 32, was crossing the street at night in Orange Beach, Alabama, when he was hit by a car and killed.

Police investigators determined that McCall was to blame for his own death. "It appears that the pedestrian stepped in front of the driver," the police said. McCall's blood-alcohol level was .304 percent, or about four times the legal limit for drivers in Alabama.

There was no evidence that the car's driver, Alexander Kimbrell, 18, had been using alcohol or drugs, and police closed the case.

Not so fast! McCall's mother, Pat Turner, sensed an opportunity: She sued Kimbrell for $3 million—$1 million each for his "negligence, wantonness and failure to exercise reasonable care" in the accident. Since Kimbrell was a teen at the time of the accident, his father has also been named in the suit.

Many may think this is kind of a humdrum outrage, but there is, of course, a twist: What gave McCall's mother the idea to file a lawsuit against the driver of a car when someone stepped in the car's path?

McCall and his mother were sued themselves in 1996 in a similar incident. McCall loaned a pickup truck owned by his mother to a friend, who ran over a pedestrian. McCall was named as a defendant in the resulting wrongful death lawsuit—as was Turner, simply because she owned the truck. Surely she was outraged at being sued like that! The case ended with a settlement, which was no doubt paid by her insurance company. Apparently, she wanted to know what the experience is like from the other side of the courtroom.

Source:

* "Accident Victim's Mother Sues Driver," *Mobile Register,* 23 February 2003

1	*	)	Location: Massachusetts
2	Grieving Parents	)	Year: 2003
3	v.	)	Award Status:
4	Innocent Driver	)	Dishonorable Mention
5		)	

DON'T WALK

Amy Woods, 14, and a friend were crossing the street in Springfield, Massachusetts. Roger O'Neil, a NYNEX telephone repairman, saw her cross the first two lanes of traffic. Fearing the girls might step right in front of him, he stopped his van so they could pass by. Indeed, aren't we all taught to stop for pedestrians?

As the girls crossed in front of him, he saw a blur in his mirror—a car coming up the next lane beside him. "I think I closed my eyes because I knew what was about to happen," O'Neil said.

Postal clerk Jeffrey Felix was taking his wife to the bookstore. He didn't see either girl until he hit Amy. "It looked like she jumped on my hood," he said.

Amy was severely injured. Seven years later, she is unable to take care of herself, walk, or even communicate. She lives in a rehabilitation hospital.

Because Amy was crossing in front of the van, Felix was unable to see her until she popped out in front of him—without looking, witnesses said. Yet Amy's parents, Kay and Gary Woods, sued him anyway. The case against Felix was settled.

End of the story? Not when there are other pools of money lying around. This is, after all, the Stella Awards!

NYNEX, now part of Verizon, is a big company with big pockets. But just a second: NYNEX repairman O'Neil *stopped* for Amy! How could he or his employer have any portion of the blame for what happened to her? Because, her parents claim, he waved at Amy to cross in front of him. O'Neil says no, he absolutely *did not* motion to Amy to cross, let alone somehow communicate that she could step into the next lane without looking. The driver behind him says he saw O'Neil wave the girls by, but he, from his poor vantage point, was the only witness to report it.

Even if he did wave her by, how would that make him responsible for her safety for the duration of her crossing? Would that mean that every time any driver—*you*, for instance—motions to another, you are taking responsibility for what happens when that person moves forward without looking?

By their lawsuit, Kay and Gary Woods certainly seem to think so.

Massachusetts Superior Court Judge C. Brian McDonald threw the lawsuit out, saying there was no evidence Amy saw O'Neil wave her along or, if she had, that she "relied" on it to reasonably believe it was safe to continue on. But the state appeals court overturned McDonald's decision. "We cannot rule as a matter of law that his signal to the girls could only be interpreted as allowing them to pass in front of his van or that his duty to the girls extended no further than the front of his van," wrote Appeals Court Justice Scott J. Kafker in his opinion. The court has ordered the lower court to let a jury decide the issue.

Obviously the accident was tragic; that's not the issue.

This is: Waving drivers or pedestrians along is a courtesy. It indicates to them that you see them and you're letting them go before you go. It does not mean that you vouch for every other driver on the road, nor does it mean they don't have to watch where they're going. The Woodses want to take that courtesy away. If they win, drivers would be insane to take on such a responsibility for anyone, adult or child. Out goes courtesy; in comes "everyone for themselves"—a legal reinforcement of selfishness. That turns Amy's tragedy into society's tragedy.

Source:

* "Jury to Decide Liability in Accident," *Boston Globe,* 22 June 2003

 **Enough Lawyers?**

The American Bar Association compiles statistics each year on how many lawyers there are. Some states report estimates, others an exact number. As of 2003, the most recent year statistics are available, there were 1,140,622 lawyers in the fifty states plus the District of Columbia. The top ten are: California, 142,913; New York, 120,000; Illinois, 75,000; New Jersey, 70,000; Texas, 64,980; Florida, 63,400; Pennsylvania, 53,621; District of Columbia, 44,000; Massachusetts, 40,000; Virginia, 34,800. There are surely more by now. (*Source:* ABA)

```
1              *              )   Location: California
2         Killer Cops         )   Year: 2004
                              )
3             v.              )   Award Status: Winner of
4      Equipment Supplier      )   the 2003 Stella Award
                              )
5   ----------------------------)
```

A STUNNING SITUATION

Madera, California, police officer Marcy Noriega had arrested Everardo Torres, 24, and had him handcuffed in the back of her police cruiser. The charge was not too extreme: He was arrested "on suspicion of resisting and delaying police" as they tried to quiet down a noisy party.

Torres, however, was far from cooperative. As he sat in the back of the police car he kicked at the windows. Officer Noriega decided to subdue him with her Taser, which fires two metal pins attached to wires and then charges them with current to "stun" the target.

Amazingly, instead of pulling and shooting Torres with her Taser, Noriega said she accidentally drew her service handgun and shot him with that. The bullet ripped through his heart, liver, and right kidney, ensuring his rapid death.

The district attorney ruled the shooting accidental and did not file criminal charges against Officer Noriega, but the city admitted liability in the shooting and offered Torres's family a $350,000 settlement. In response, the family filed a claim for $10 million. When the city rejected the claim, the family filed a wrongful death suit in federal court.

Such is not what Stella Awards are made of, however—complaining that a professionally trained police officer mistook her firearm for a nonlethal stun gun to shoot someone in her custody is not frivolous. Rather, it's what the city said next: Officer Noriega isn't at fault for killing Torres! Not the way she and the city see things, anyway. While they admit they were "partially responsible for the loss" of Torres's life, she and the city of Madera have filed suit against Taser International, Inc., the manufacturer of the nonlethal weapon.

The lawsuit's reasoning maintains Taser is responsible for Torres's death because the company's training procedures do not adequately teach police officers the difference between the Taser and their own handguns. The company, the suit says, "provided related training and representations in such a manner so as to cause any reasonable police officer to mistakenly draw and fire a handgun instead of the Taser device."

Got that? "Any reasonable police officer" could pull the wrong gun and kill a suspect he or she merely mean to stun! Considering the thousands of police officers in the U.S. and how long Tasers have been on the market—coupled with the dubious "fact" that "any reasonable police officer" is likely "to mistakenly draw and fire a handgun instead of the Taser device"—there must be hundreds of cases of just that happening, right?

Wrong. In their research, Madera's lawyers found just two previous cases of such mistakes, though both times the unfortunate victims survived. "Once we found the two other incidents, we made [a] change" in Madera police procedure, advising officers not to carry their Taser on the same side of their belts as their handguns, says the city's lawyer. (Remember! The gun on left to stun, the one on the right to kill. Got it? Good! Back out on the streets, guys!)

The suit says Taser was "aware" its training methods were flawed, and had "a duty" to inform police departments of the risk that a trained professional might grab the wrong gun. The suit asks that Taser pay whatever amount the Torres family wins from their wrongful death lawsuit.

Cops have incredibly stressful, important jobs. To get that job done they're given astounding powers, up to and including the legal right to kill citizens who are threatening others. With those powers come similarly awesome responsibilities, such as carefully preserving suspects' rights and knowing when—and how—to use the various weapons at their disposal. For Madera and Officer Noriega to stand up in public to say "any reasonable police officer" doesn't know the difference between a nonlethal weapon and a handgun is an insult to every professional peace officer—and an abdication of the responsibility that has been placed on them. Torres was likely not a choirboy, but his death is a tragic accident, and shouldn't be treated as an opportunity for the city to try to pin the blame on an equipment supplier.

Source:

* "Madera Sues Taser Maker," *Fresno Bee,* 29 July 2003

1	*	) Location: Ohio
2	Shocked Family	) Year: 2003
3	v.	) Award Status: Runner-up
4	Amusement Park	) for the 2003 Stella Award
5		)

I SEE THE LIGHT?

Shawn Perkins of Laurel, Indiana, took his family to Paramount's Kings Island Amusement Park in Mason, Ohio, on June 12, 2001. As they left the park to go to their car, a thunderstorm was approaching. As the family reached the car, lightning struck and "the car [Perkins] was touching was blown apart," claims the family's lawyer, Drake Ebner.

Oh, no! A *lawyer* for a lightning strike? Yep. This was no "act of God. That would be a lot of people's knee-jerk reaction in these types of situations, frankly," Ebner said, clearly expecting criticism over the suit. He said the amusement park had "a duty of ordinary care" to warn visitors of any foreseeable danger, and the Perkinses were not warned about the storm. The amusement park "could have told the people not to go to their cars," he said, "which are large metal objects that can attract lightning." (Lawyers have to be careful to define every term they use. They have to justify their big fees somehow, and I'll bet you never thought that was the definition of a car. See? He's a professional; don't try this at home!)

"A lot of voltage passed through his brain," Ebner said. His suit, filed in Hamilton County (Ohio) Common Pleas

Court, says that as a result of the lightning strike, Perkins is suffering from brain damage, which has resulted in a "cognitive deficit and severe memory loss." Perhaps not surprisingly, Ebner noted Perkins also has a fear of being outside.

"We believe that the weather system was predictable," Ebner continued, building his case step by step. "Therefore, the risk and injury to Mr. Perkins was predictable and therefore avoidable." If the park didn't know about the storm, he added, it should have known, perhaps by subscribing to a weather prediction service. "If you are a multimillion-dollar business, wouldn't you?" Ebner asked. However, he quickly added, "I'm just not mentioning [the park's multimillion-dollar gross income] for the concept of deep pockets for the suit." Oh, no—perish the thought! Such a thing *never* entered our minds. (Really! We swear! May lightning—well . . . strike that idea.)

"Think of the amount of money Kings Island spends to get people to the park," he said, still lingering on the money issue. "Safety is not common sense." It's not? No, he said: "You and I don't run amusement parks." (Speak for yourself, chum.) "Because they are in the unique situation they are in—that says they need to do things that you and I don't do." Like, say, know to take cover in a thunderstorm?

Sources:

* "Family Sues Kings Island," *Cincinnati Post,* 17 June 2003
* "Kings Island Sued by Family," *Cincinnati Enquirer,* 19 June 2003

Ohio

Ohio is a nice, quiet, middle-America state. And, according to the Ohio Citizens Against Lawsuit Abuse, frivolous cases cost the state $8,200,323,061 per year. Divided among the state's estimated population of 11,373,541, each man, woman, and child in the state is hit with a hidden lawsuit "tax" of $721 per year. (*Source: OCALA Web site*)

```
1              *              )   Location: Massachusetts
                              )
2     Grieving Parents        )   Year: 2003
                              )
3             v.              )   Award Status:
                              )   Dishonorable Mention
4         Tow Truck           )
                              )
5  ---------------------------)
```

BY HOOK OR BY CROOK

Melissa Gosule called upon AAA, formerly known as the American Automobile Association, when her car broke down on Cape Cod, Massachusetts. A tow truck arrived, but when driver John Cubellis learned she wanted to be towed all the way to Boston, sixty miles away, he told Gosule he was too busy to be gone that long and she would have to wait three to four hours before he could take her.

He left Gosule at her car, but it was hardly in the middle of nowhere: She was in a busy parking lot surrounded by restaurants, a gas station, and a fire station. But Gosule, 27, apparently decided not to wait, and instead accepted a ride from a passerby, Michael Gentile.

Eight days later, Gosule's body was found in a shallow grave. She had been raped. Gentile was convicted of her murder.

But finding out who was responsible for Gosule's death—and seeing him convicted and imprisoned for life—was far from enough for her parents, Leslie Gosule and Sandra Glaser, or her stepfather, Peter Glaser. "Had AAA done what they tell the world they do—provide reliable and reasonable emergency roadside assistance—

Melissa would still be with us," Leslie Gosule said. The trio filed suit against AAA; its regional organization, AAA Southern New England; and Cubellis, the tow truck driver, seeking unspecified damages.

The wrongful death suit claims AAA, which has more than forty-six million members in North America and dispatches help to about thirty million motorists per year, was "negligent" in not doing more for Gosule. "AAA is not who they say they are," her father complains. Legal observers say it's the first case of its kind.

Let's hope it's the last, because here's the kicker: Gosule wasn't even a member of AAA. When she broke down she called her stepfather, Peter Glaser (who you might remember is one of the people who sued), and he was the one who called AAA. Yet the "Benefit Guide" for members notes that members are covered "in a [*sic*] eligible vehicle in which you are riding or driving." It certainly does *not* cover other people in their own cars when the member isn't even present—AAA's guide notes that "roadside assistance benefits are not transferable." Yet the AAA driver went out anyway, provided her service, and agreed to the lengthy tow, despite all of this. Still, her family calls this level of service "negligent."

On the third day of the trial, AAA, not wanting the bad publicity of fighting a murder victim's grieving parents in court, gave the parents an "undisclosed settlement" to drop the case. Here's an idea to reduce the outrageous abuse of courts, which you should remember are a branch of the government (and by definition the government is "of the people, by the people, and for the people"—or, if you will, "owned" by the people): Once a lawsuit is filed in court, there should be no secret settlements. You want to use our courts to get justice? Fine, that's what they're there for. But if you want the people to enforce justice, the people should have a right to know the outcome of the action. The settlement should be part of the open court record for anyone to see.

Sadly, AAA considered it politic to settle. Awarding outrageous behavior with cash only does one thing: It encourages the same sort of behavior. By settling, insurance companies, including AAA, simply invite more of the same.

Sources:

* "Kin Sue AAA in Slaying of Massachusetts Woman," Associated Press, 9 September 2003
* "Family Settles Suit Against AAA, Driver," *Boston Globe*, 11 September 2003

Petty Squabbles
We Need a Jury for <u>This</u>?

Saying "I'm sorry" and making amends ought to be good enough in petty arguments—unless attorneys use that as evidence of liability. Either way, sometimes even the smallest arguments end up in court.

```
1              *              )  Location: New York
                              )
2          Neighbor          )  Year: 2002
                              )
3             v.             )  Award Status:
                              )  Dishonorable Mention
4          Neighbor          )
                              )
5  -------------------------- )
```

A GOOD FENCE MAKES
A GOOD NEIGHBOR

Michael and Laura Schek have some eye-catching decorations in the yard of their Patterson, New York, home. Pink flamingos abound—fifty-eight of them. One group of the gaudy plastic birds sits around a "picnic table" made from old truck tires, "drinking" from pink plastic cups glued to the table.

A fake Christmas tree, wrapped in a white sheet, sits by the driveway. Then there's the toilet on a stack of wooden pallets; on the toilet sits a gargoyle. And it's all capped by a sign that reads, "Our dog can run to this fence in 2.8 seconds, can you?"

It's too much for neighbor Tyler Murello, who owns a forty-one-acre lot next door. He has to get to his property via the Scheks' driveway, which is allowed by a legal easement. But that means he has to drive by the Scheks' on the way to his lot, where he is building a house. The four-bedroom, 4,500-square-foot "spectacular mountain-top estate" he's building also has a separate 1,100-square-foot caretaker's cottage. The property is listed for sale for $1.35 million.

Murello says the Scheks are decorating their yard this way on purpose in an attempt to "repulse" anyone looking to buy the house. The Scheks had previously sued Murello in an attempt to block the construction, but the lawsuit failed and building went ahead. About that time is when the yard decorations popped up, which the Scheks say is simply a manifestation of their freedom of expression.

"We find it somewhat unusual that this sudden artistic inspiration should occur in a matter of days after the resolution of the previous litigation," said Robert Lusardi, Murello's attorney.

The Scheks' lawyer Mitchell Lieberman said their decorations are meant to "deter trespassing construction workers" and slow down the construction vehicles going up and down the driveway. "When pricing a fence, it was in the tens of thousands of dollars," Lieberman said. "The upper crust of Putnam society may not appreciate these lawn ornaments, [but] my clients don't have a problem with them," he said. "In the meantime, their First Amendment rights are being trashed."

So, this is a freedom of speech issue? "Mr. Murello's tastes and my clients' tastes are obviously different," Lieberman said. "We're not pink flamingo specialists but we do a lot of First Amendment work."

Pfui, Murello says. He has sued the Scheks, asking for $8 million.

Dennis Plante, president of Union Products, Inc., in Leominster, Massachusetts ("The Home of the Original World Famous Pink Lawn Flamingo"), said this is the first time he's heard of someone suing over his lawn ornaments. The company has been selling the plastic birds since 1957. The company sells six hundred thousand of the things per year. But that didn't impress New York

Supreme Court Justice S. Barrett Hickman, who granted
Murello a temporary restraining order demanding the re-
moval of the Scheks' yard art. A hearing has been scheduled to determine the next step.

There has to be a Stella Award in here somewhere, but
is it due to Murello, for suing his neighbor for $8 million
because the Scheks' fifty-eight pink plastic flamingos and
other assorted "art" are making million-dollar homes look
like they've been placed in a trailer park? Or is it due to
the Scheks, for trying to stop a man from building a house
on his own property, first using the courts and, when that
failed, with pink guerrilla tactics? Or maybe it's both, in
recognition of the sort of argument one would expect
from a pair of squabbling children?

It ain't easy being a juror in the Court of Public Opinion.

When neighbors don't get along, they can sit down and
talk out their differences. But that ignores the New American Dream of "something for nothing," so let's step into
the courtroom and not only vex our next-door pest, but
rake in a few million in the process! While it sounds pretty
stupid, perhaps it's better than them dueling with pistols
at the bottom of the driveway. But only just barely.

Source:

★ "Plastic Bird Art Inspires $8 Million Suit," *White Plains
  Journal News,* 9 November 2002

```
1              *          )   Location: Connecticut
2          Secretary      )   Year: 2002
3             v.           )   Award Status:
4         Her Employer     )   Dishonorable Mention
5                          )
```

WHEN A PENNY SAVED IS
NOT A PENNY EARNED

Rosemary Aquavia, a secretary for the mayor of Naugatuck, Connecticut, was reprimanded by her supervisor—orally, not even in writing—after she was caught using a borough fax machine for a personal matter.

Rather than accept the rebuke for breaking the rules, Aquavia filed a federal lawsuit against the town for violating her First Amendment right to free speech.

The case actually made it to trial. A jury of Aquavia's peers agreed that the slap on her hand was too harsh a penalty, and awarded her monetary damages. The total amount awarded by the sympathetic jury: one cent.

Aquavia appealed the reward to U.S. District Court Judge Janet Arterton, asking her to increase her damages—to one dollar. (Yes, really.) The judge turned down the appeal.

The case took three years from incident to the end of her appeal, and cost Aquavia $5,000 in legal fees. While amusing, think of the costs to the town and the federal government, since the case was heard in federal court. That means *you* paid for Aquavia's tantrum to be heard.

Source:

* "Penny's Worth of Justice Is All She Gets," *Waterbury Republican-American,* 23 September 2002

```
1              *              )  Location: Illinois
2   Passenger in Accident     )  Year: 2004
                              )
3           v.                )  Award Status: Winner of
                              )  the 2004 Stella Award
4        The Car              )
5                            )
```

CLICK-IT OR TICKET

Mary Ubaudi of Madison County, Illinois, says William Humphrey was driving too fast, and perhaps she should know: She was a passenger in his car. When they got to a construction zone, Humphrey lost control and flipped the auto. Ubaudi was thrown from the vehicle and, her attorney J. Michael Weilmuenster says, sustained severe and life-threatening injuries.

Ubaudi has sued Humphrey, asking for "at least $50,000" in damages. Surely if he was driving too fast for road conditions—such as in a construction zone—and caused an accident, he should be liable. And indeed, that wouldn't make news in the True Stella Awards. But Ubaudi's attorney didn't want to stop there—not if there were some potentially deep pockets to pick.

The lawsuit, filed in Madison County Circuit Court, thus also names Rowe Construction for "at least $50,000," because it was under state contract to do the construction work on the roadway. Ubaudi claims the company "failed to provide proper and reasonably safe traffic-control devices for road construction, failed to properly maintain the public highway in a safe and navigable condition during the road project and failed to provide guardrails or railings during the construction project."

OK, maybe that's plausible. But that's still not a deep enough pocket. So Ubaudi and her attorney have also named Mazda Motors, the manufacturer of Humphrey's car, a Miata. And what, pray tell, did they do wrong? The suit claims the company "failed to provide instructions regarding the safe and proper use of a seatbelt."

One hopes Mazda's attorneys make her swear in court that she has never before worn a seatbelt, has never flown on an airliner, and that she's too stupid to figure out how to fasten a seatbelt. Meanwhile, her suit demands "in excess of $150,000" from the automaker, setting their liability at more than three times what she thinks the driver should be on the hook for.

Source:

* "Driver, Road Contractor, Auto Maker Sued in Accident," *Madison County Record,* 18 November 2004

You Have Been Warned!

A "Wacky Warning Label Contest" is conducted anually by Michigan Lawsuit Abuse Watch "to reveal how lawsuits, and concern about lawsuits, have created a need for commonsense warnings on products." Some of the ridiculous legal warnings found on American products include:

- "Do not use for personal hygiene"—on a toilet brush.
- "This product moves when used"—on a child's scooter.
- "Never remove food or other items from the blades while the product is operating"—on an electric blender.
- "Remove child before folding"—on a baby stroller.
- "If you do not understand, or cannot read, all directions, cautions and warnings, do not use this product"—on a bottle of drain cleaner.
- "Do not use the Silence Feature in emergency situations. It will not extinguish a fire"—on a smoke detector.
- "Caution: Risk of Fire"—on a fireplace log.

"Warning labels are a sign of our lawsuit-plagued times," says M-LAW's president, Robert Dorigo Jones. M-LAW's Web site allows readers to submit stupid warning labels. (*Source: mlaw.org*)

1	*	) Location: California
2	Opportunists	) Year: 2002
3	v.	) Award Status:
4	Their Personal	) Dishonorable Mention
5	Organizer	)

PALMED OFF

Advertising for Palm, Inc.'s m130 said the handheld computer supports "more than 65,000 colors." Oops: It actually "only" supports 58,621 colors. Would anyone be able to tell the difference?

It doesn't matter. "The company is working on a plan to compensate customers," announced a company spokeswoman, but they're too late: A lawsuit has already been filed—and given class-action status—alleging the missing 6,380 or so colors demonstrates Palm's "unfair competition, and fraudulent, unfair, deceptive and false advertising."

No wonder litigation is so expensive: You have to pay the lawyers to count!

Once it discovered the mistake, the company started to work toward fixing it. But that wasn't good enough for lawyers who could only see the potential for grabbing a big fee by jumping in where they weren't needed.

Source:

* "Suit: Palm Overstates Color Feature," Associated Press, 27 August 2002

```
1              *            )  Location: New York
                            )
2      Theme Restaurant     )  Year: 2003
                            )
3            v.             )  Award Status:
                            )  Dishonorable Mention
4     Unimpressed Diners    )
                            )
5  ------------------------ )
```

EVERYBODY WANTS TO
BE A CRITIC

Restaurants usually love reviewers. Business can skyrocket on a good—or even mediocre—review. But what if the review turns out to be bad? In America, the restaurant sues.

Lucky Cheng's, in Manhattan's East Village, features a bit of shtick with their steak. The waiters—men—dress as women, for instance.

In its "opinionated, witty and no-holds-barred" review, the popular restaurant guide from Zagat opined, "God knows 'you don't go for the food' at this East Village-Asian Eclectic. Rather you go to 'gawk' at the 'hilarious cross-dressing' staff who 'tell dirty jokes,' perform 'impromptu floor shows' and 'offer lap dances for dessert.' " It offered a score of 9 for the food—but that's out of 30 possible points.

People "don't go to the restaurant for its food"? That's not definitude, that's defamation, the restaurant said. It filed a suit in Manhattan Supreme Court saying it was "libelously attacked" in Zagat's review, which "falsely state[s] the quality of food and beverage, service, wait staff, sanitation and cleanliness are substandard and unworthy of patronage." The owners claim that the review, published in October 2003, did not take into account improvements in the food since the restaurant came under new management in April 2003.

Thus, those new owners asked the court to award it $10 million, plus $250,000 for loss of reputation and goodwill, plus $30,000 per week in lost revenue starting October 14, 2003, when Zagat published its 2004 guide. They argued Zagat should have checked the low score assigned to its food to ensure accuracy. (What, they're expected to eat that stuff more than once?)

Unlike many review services, Zagat does not rely on a particular person, but rather "hundreds or thousands" of patrons who turn in ratings to the company. The ratings cover food, atmosphere, and service. Their previous year's guide gave the restaurant a food rating of 8, so a 9 actually represents a 12.5 percent improvement. Isn't it more likely, then, that the restaurant's supposed reduction in business is more a reflection of the new management's actions than the result of a single, improved review?

In response to the suit, a Zagat spokeswoman said the company is "confident of our review of Lucky Cheng's, and we stand by it. This is the collective opinion of the contributors." The spokeswoman noted the company has been sued three times before; two of those suits have been dismissed.

Reviews are not statements of fact, they're opinion. And where would we be without the ability to express it without retribution? Courts have consistently held that the publication of opinion, including product reviews, is protected free speech. If you told someone you didn't like a restaurant's food, should they be able to turn you in for a reward? Should TSA be sued because we expressed the *opinion* that this is a silly and overblown example of lawsuits gone nuts? Because, in our considered opinion, that's exactly what it is.

Sources:

* "Transvestite Eatery Sues Zagat," Reuters, 25 December 2003.
* "Cabaret-Restaurant Sues Zagat over Food Rating," Associated Press, 24 December 2003

Afterword:

Judge Diane Lebedeff tossed the suit in August 2004, ruling, "A restaurant review, no matter how harsh, is not an appropriate basis for a libel action because it reflects an individual's subjective opinion about the quality of food, service and decor." Elapsed time: not quite a year.

Source:

* "Court rejects restaurant's libel claim vs. Zagat," *Nation's Restaurant News*, 30 August 2004

```
1            *            )  Location: Maine
                          )
2      Unwanted Man       )  Year: 2004
                          )
3           v.            )  Award Status:
                          )  Dishonorable Mention
4    Convenience Store    )
                          )
5   ----------------------)
```

GRAVE MISTAKE

Brad Graves and Ronald Hicks are both lifelong residents of Etna, Maine, population 1,000. Using his computer, Hicks made a joke "wanted poster" featuring a photo of Graves; it identified him as "Abdul Graves, suspected leader of the outlaw organization Extreme Activist Terrorism Militia of Etna" (or "EATME") and posted it on the cash register at the Country Corner Variety store for one day. Rather than laugh, Graves tore it down—and called his lawyer.

Attorney Brett Baber said Graves was "mortified" by being called a terrorist. "In this day and age, anytime one is alleged to be a terrorist and part of a terrorist group, it does inherent damage to one's reputation," Baber said, helping justify his filing a lawsuit against Hicks in Penobscot County Superior Court. The suit seeks "reasonable" compensatory and punitive damages, plus costs. "Reasonable"? Like, maybe, two bits?

Source:

* "Etna Man Sues over Fake Wanted Poster," *Bangor Daily News,* 16 July 2004

```
1              *              )   Location: Florida
                              )
2        Food Critic          )   Year: 2003
                              )
3            v.               )   Award Status:
                              )   Dishonorable Mention
4      Advice Columnist       )
                              )
5    ---------------------------)
```

FOOD FIGHT

D oris Reynolds, the food columnist for the *Naples Daily News* newspaper in Florida, apparently has a lot of personal problems. So much so that she has been seeking advice and guidance from the same newspaper's "spiritual advice" columnist, Angela Passidomo Trafford.

Since 1999, Reynolds had been getting "spiritual self-healing treatment" from Trafford, and got spiritual advice from her for three years before that. In those seven or so years, Reynolds said, she paid Trafford between $2 million and $3 million for her services.

Reynolds said she paid Trafford $500,000 in 2002 alone, and the "spiritual healing sessions" were spent talking, meditating, and drawing. The two women met up to seven days a week for their four- to five-hour sessions, for which Reynolds paid $190 per hour at the start, a fee that eventually hit $380 per hour.

But in April 2003, she alleged, things got ugly. She said Trafford "demanded" $150,000 for future services. When Reynolds said she didn't have that much cash, Trafford visited her at home and "demanded" a check for $95,000, marked as a "gift" so that "she wouldn't have to pay income tax" on the money. Reynolds wrote the check, but "it was under extreme duress," she said. "She said she would not come back and treat me unless I gave her that money." Reynolds said she "needed help" to deal with depression, anxiety, stress, and an unhappy marriage. "I became dependent on her," she said. But Trafford "terminated her treatment" a month after the $95,000 payment "without explanation or reason."

Well, if your spiritual adviser fails you, where do you turn? To your legal adviser.

Reynolds has sued Trafford in Collier County Circuit Court for at least $1 million, accusing her of constructive fraud, unjust enrichment, and civil theft. Further, the suit alleges Trafford received payment for services she never provided, and that Trafford "intentionally misrepresented to Reynolds that she was a messenger of God and Reynolds needed to pay her."

"I have always tried to find spiritual solutions in my life," she said. "I trusted her. This is not easy for me. I'm not doing this for money. I'm doing this because I think people should be accountable for the harm they cause me."

"There's no truth in this," Trafford said. "It's just an unbelievable situation." In her formal response to the lawsuit, she denied all charges and said the $95,000 was, indeed, a gift.

As for the *Daily News*, managing editor William Blanton said he plans to continue to run both women's columns. But let's hope they're not on the same page.

Source:

* "Food Columnist Suing Spiritual Advice Columnist for More than $1m," *Naples Daily News,* 25 July 2003

Afterword:

Readers—especially journalists, who are intimately familiar with the low wages paid at newspapers—wondered where a columnist would get $2 million to $3 million to pay for "spiritual counseling" alone. The only clue I could find was that one of the problems she went to the spiritualist for was her "unhappy marriage." I'm guessing there's a positive feedback loop involved there. . . .

Others called the psychic healer's actions fraud. "It seems that it's perfectly OK for religions to defraud believers with unproven and specious claims, so long as they do so on a regular basis and in smaller amounts, but when someone gets greedy and uses beliefs to collect large sums of money, they are suddenly frauds—yet countless other preachers use the spiritual dependency of followers to sway their voting, their lives, and exert influence. I think we need to develop consistency in how our laws treat claims made by religion/ists with other business claims. If a company claims its product will cure your warts, and it doesn't work, you're entitled to a refund, and if it is discovered that the company knew it didn't work but promised results anyway, they can be prosecuted for fraud. Why not hold religious claims to the same standard?"

Interestingly, the reader was in a sense arguing my point. When people give money to their legitimate, mainstream church (however you'd like to define that), we don't expect something in return or demand the money back if whatever "miracle" we're hoping/praying for doesn't come through. Mrs. Reynolds freely chose her spiritual path, and now wants a jury to second-guess her own decisions. How is that reasonable?

```
1                *              )   Location: New York
2       Resident of Crime-      )   Year: 2004
                                )
3       Ridden Community        )   Award Status: Runner-up
                                )   for the 2004 Stella Award
4              v.               )
                                )
5       Her Phone Bill          )
                                )
```

IT OUGHT TO BE A CRIME

Tanisha Torres, 26, stopped frequently at the Radio Shack store at the Airport Plaza mall in Farmingdale, New York, to pay her cell phone bill. Torres, from Wyandanch, on Long Island, noticed that her town was listed on her computer-generated receipt from the store as "Crimedanch," not "Wyndanch."

The first time, she thought it was a mistake. But it happened again and again, because it was entered into Radio Shack's computer that way.

Why "Crimedanch"? The moniker is a common nickname for the community among people who know the area—like, say, the cops in town. Wyndanch "is one of our busier areas" for crimes such as drug-dealing and prostitution, confirmed Inspector James Rhoads, the commanding officer of the Suffolk police precinct that covers the township. "It takes a lot of our attention."

"I'm not a criminal," Torres complained. "My son plays on the high school football team." (Um, *huh*?) "I was raised there and I am proud of my community." She said she was "outraged" by having her town's name mistyped on her receipt. "That's embarrassing."

What, she hasn't heard the joke name before? Sure, she said. But, she complained, "I have to go through this every day. But then I go to make a payment on a bill and it was just the end."

It's a good thing to be proud of your hometown, to be sure. So did she complain to the store and ask them to correct the entry in their computer? Did she tell Radio Shack she is proud of her town and didn't appreciate the joke? Certainly not! This is America! One doesn't complain, one doesn't ask for corrections, one doesn't suffer from "outrage" or "embarrassment"—at least not at the hands of some big company with a lot of money. One sues as a first resort.

The store's manager had no idea the receipt was wrong. When a New York *Newsday* reporter called manager Bill Sullivan to check after hearing of Torres's plight, Sullivan called up Torres's record from the computer and found the joke spelling. He checked to see who had entered it that way: It was an employee who was no longer there. A spokeswoman for Radio Shack's headquarters told the newspaper, "As soon as we were alerted to the situation, we changed it in the system, and immediately rectified the situation." As simple as that—and as no doubt they would have if Torres had complained to the store in the first place.

So was the store's action good enough? Nope. Torres had already taken her receipts to attorney Andrew Siben of Bay Shore, who duly filed suit against Radio Shack in New York State Supreme Court. The suit claims the store was "negligent and reckless in its operation and maintenance of the store and the receipt system, and in the hiring, supervision and monitoring of employees." It begs unspecified damages to help Torres to get over being "embarrassed, flustered and shamed," as well as her suffering emotional distress and mental anguish. All that because the joke spelling "implicitly or explicitly labeled her a criminal," the suit says. Right: A joke that she acknowledges she hears "every day." And who had the opinion that Torres is a "criminal"? No one—no one but perhaps the people Torres showed the receipts to herself, and it's hard to believe even they would do anything but chuckle at the joke.

Nope, Siben said. "Clearly, it is defamatory to Ms. Torres and the entire community. It's a violation of civil rights to be characterized in a way that infers that everyone from Wyndanch is a criminal."

Hey, maybe Siben does have a point. Just consider how a few opportunistic, sue-for-anything attorneys lead the public at large to infer all lawyers are slimy, money-grubbing criminals! Where should the suit filed in Court of Public Opinion be served on you, Mr. Siben?

Source:

* "No Writing Off This Receipt," *Newsday,* 4 February 2004

```
1                    *              )   Location: New Mexico
                                    )
2    Supermarket Employees         )   Year: 2004
                                    )
3              v.                   )   Award Status:
                                    )   Dishonorable Mention
4          Bicycle Pants            )
                                    )
5   --------------------------------)
```

WE CAN ALL SEE RIGHT
THROUGH THIS ONE

A group of female employees at the Whole Foods Market in Santa Fe, New Mexico, said that in 2000 a customer walked into the store wearing white, see-through bicycle shorts—without underwear. They said they complained to the manager, but the manager failed to throw the customer out of the store.

A short time later one of the women, Maria Bautista, was fired. That was because, the store's manager said, she had told other employees it was permissible to misuse employee discount cards. Then a second woman, Cindy Medrano, said she was "sexually harassed" by having to see the man in the shorts, but says the store didn't do anything about it. A third, Vasti Aguilar, jumped in and said she was a diabetic, and the store didn't accommodate her needs for breaks to tend to her illness. And a fourth, Jeannie Leyba, said she was pregnant and the store "forced" her to quit.

A lot of unrelated charges, to be sure, but their chain of complaints apparently fell like dominoes after the incident with the man in the shorts. They said the store's failure to prevent the man from being in their view was negligent, and Bautista said it was her complaint about seeing the man that resulted in her being fired, not any improper actions on her part.

The women thus banded together and sued the supermarket chain for "hundreds of thousands of dollars" in compensatory and punitive damages, claiming the store had violated New Mexico's Human Rights Act because its managers "fostered" an "environment of discrimination and sexual harassment" by allowing customers to walk around wearing what they considered too-thin clothing—and that caused them emotional distress. They also alleged "negligent supervision" by managers, and Bautista added she suffered post-traumatic stress disorder for having to deal with the white-shorted man without the managers' help.

The poor dears.

They still got their day in Santa Fe District Court—eight days, actually. But after the trial, the jury decided they didn't buy the women's arguments. The jury found Bautista's firing justified; it found Medrano never made any formal complaint regarding sexual harassment for the store to take action on; and it found the store indeed accommodated Aguilar's diabetic condition by giving her the breaks from work she needed. The jury deadlocked, however, on Leyba's pregnancy argument, with six jurors accepting her version of the story and six agreeing with store managers that they indeed worked hard to give her less strenuous job assignments. Judge Carol Vigil ruled she could try her case again if she wished.

"We're going to appeal," Bautista said after the verdicts were handed down. When asked about the appeal, the women's attorney, George Geran, would only say, "Miss Bautista is speaking for herself."

Employers have a duty to provide a proper work environment and to accommodate employees' medical conditions. But they certainly don't have a duty to evaluate the fashion statements that various customers wish to make, even if they're in poor taste, and cover the eyes of adult employees who might object.

More significantly, using a clueless customer as an excuse to label oneself a victim of "sexual harassment" is a slap in the face of countless women (and some men) who suffer *real* sexual harassment in the workplace, such as unwanted advances from someone who holds the keys to their professional future. The sight of an inappropriately dressed moron deserves a snicker, not a crass lineup at a trough of cash while falsely crying, "I'm a victim."

Either the man's attire was legal or it was not. And if not, it's not up to the store's manager to confront the lawbreaker, it's up to the police—and the women could have called the police just as easily as the manager could, and sooner if they had to track him down to ask. So who, again, committed any error by not calling the cops? You guessed it: the plaintiffs.

Total time from shorts to getting the short end: a little over three years.

Sources:

* "Workers Suing Over Man in See-Through Shorts," Reuters newswire, 19 March 2004
* "3 Ex-workers Lose Whole Foods Case," *Global Diversity @ Work,* April 2004

It's My Right!
The Infinite Expansion of the Constitution

If there's one thing Americans know, it's that they have *rights*. Courts have backed an ever-expanding number of those "rights," no matter that they were never spelled out in the Constitution. But if there's one thing Americans like to forget, it's that for every "right" there is a corresponding "responsibility." And if that right just isn't in the Constitution, no matter: We know our rights when we see them violated, even if no one else does, and doesn't that justify a petty lawsuit?

```
1                *              )   Location: Washington
2         Sports Boor          )   Year: 2002
                               )
3              v.              )   Award Status:
4        Baseball Team          )   Dishonorable Mention
                               )
5    ----------------------------)
```

HAD THE FEVER AND
HAD IT BAD

Anthony Ercolano, 44, is a fan of the Seattle Mariners baseball team. A big, *big* fan. The former Microsoft employee has a pair of season tickets to the exclusive "Diamond Club" section right behind home plate. They cost him $32,000.

"He's loud," said the Mariners' attorney, Bruce Johnson. "That's the gist of it." Very loud. And, apparently, very constant. He shouts at short players to "stand up." He makes baby-crying sounds when batters argue with the umpire. On and on. And since he's just five rows behind home plate, they hear him—and so do the other fans nearby.

Mariners Executive Vice President Bob Aylward called Ercolano on the phone to ask him to tone it down or move farther from the action. Johnson says the Mariners "have full authority to protect nearby fans in the Diamond Club from the heavy, incessant volume of noise created by Mr. Ercolano" and that the team is "rightly concerned for the well-being and comfort of their fans, including those in the Diamond Club. . . . These fans do not come to the ballpark to be repeatedly and constantly assaulted by Mr. Ercolano's noise."

But since Ercolano said, "I believe in being loud at a baseball game," he would have none of these suggestions. Incensed at being hushed, even in private, he sued the team in King County Superior Court claiming that the baseball franchise is violating his freedom of speech and "possibly breaching his season-ticket contract." His suit asks for a guarantee he will not be ejected from any game and that his season tickets will not be revoked, and, of course, he wants an unspecified amount of monetary damages.

"Really, what he wants is to be free of harassment," said Paul Meiklejohn, Ercolano's attorney. "And he'd like an apology from the Mariners." He said his client's enjoyment of baseball is the "game and cheering and teaching his [daughters] about the game." But perhaps even more, Ercolano "feels that he spent a lot of money for these tickets . . . and he didn't expect to be belittled."

Funny, but isn't that pretty much what the Mariners are saying?

Source:

* "Fan Sues after Team Tells Him to Shut up," *Seattle Times,* 28 August 2002

```
1            *            )   Location: Massachusetts
2      Holey Woman        )   Year: 2002
                          )
3           v.            )   Award Status:
                          )   Dishonorable Mention
4        Employer         )
                          )
5   ----------------------- )
```

PUTTING HER FAITH IN
THE COURT SYSTEM

Kimberly M. Cloutier, 27, of West Springfield, Massachusetts, has several piercings in each ear for earrings. And a lip ring. And an eyebrow ring. In the spring of 2001 her employer, Costco Wholesale, operator of the Costco warehouse stores, instituted a new dress code. Among other things, it prohibits facial and tongue jewelry, and visible tattoos.

Although Cloutier had worn her jewelry for more than two years during her four-year Costco career, the new dress code made her multiple piercings a problem. Store managers told her she had to cover or remove her "facial jewelry" while at work, but when she refused she was sent home. After several weeks at an impasse, she was fired.

This being America and all, Cloutier responded by filing a lawsuit against Costco in U.S. District Court in Springfield. She doesn't claim some hazy violation of her freedom of expression; rather, Cloutier says, her piercings are a sign of her faith, and Costco's actions constitute religious discrimination. She is asking for $2 million in compensation.

What makes her body piercings a religious issue? Cloutier said she is a member of the "Church of Body

Modification," which calls itself "an interfaith church whose members practice an assortment of ancient body modification rites, which we believe are essential to our spiritual salvation." She was emboldened in her claim by the U.S. Equal Employment Opportunity Commission. When Cloutier complained of Costco's actions, EEOC Boston Area Director Robert L. Sanders ruled Costco "probably" violated the 1964 Civil Rights Act when it fired her.

"It's not just an aesthetic thing," Cloutier said. "It's your body; you're taking control of it." Well which is it: religious persecution or "body control"?

Her former employer, of course, disagreed that this was a religious issue. "Costco was acting in the best interest of its members and customers," said Costco attorney Lynn A. Kappelman. It's reasonable for the company to bar facial piercings "in the same way that we require our employees to be sanitary and clean and neat in our dress."

It's a typical reaction to Costco: You always come out of there with more than you intended when you went in.

Source:

* "Eyebrow Ring, Firing Spark $2 Million Suit," *Springfield Union-News*, 16 October 2002

Afterword:

Cloutier offered to remove her jewelry and wear transparent covers, but when Costco accepted that accommodation she later refused to do so. On March 30, 2004, U.S. District Judge Ponsor held that Costco's resulting "reasonable accommodation" barred them from liability, and granted summary judgment to Costco. But on Dececember 1, 2004, when the U.S. Court of Appeals for the First District affirmed that summary judgment, it did so on different grounds: that Costco had no duty to accommodate Cloutier because it couldn't do so without undue hardship. Total time from the new dress code through the end of the appeal process: more than three and a half years.

```
1               *              )  Location: Ohio
                               )
2          Skinny Guy          )  Year: 2002
                               )
3              v.              )  Award Status: Runner-up
                               )  for the 2002 Stella Award
4           Fat Guy            )
                               )
5  -------------------------------)
```

MOMMY, HE'S TOUCHING ME!

Attorney Philip Shafer of Ashland, Ohio, flew on Delta Airlines from New Orleans to Cincinnati and was given a seat, he said, next to a fat man.

"He was a huge man," Shafer said. "He and I [were] literally and figuratively married from the right kneecap to the shoulder for two hours. That's not what I paid for."

Shafer therefore "suffered embarrassment, severe discomfort, mental anguish and severe emotional distress," he claims in a lawsuit against the airline. Shafer figures this embarrassment, discomfort, mental anguish, and emotional distress could be cured by a $9,500 payment from Delta, but he's willing to settle out of court.

"Literally married"? Surely the "huge man" is ready for a divorce, and will happily settle for half of Shafer's net worth.

Source:

* "Ashland Attorney Sues over 'Jet Jam,'" *Mansfield News Journal,* 1 August 2002

```
1              *              )  Location: California
2       Little Leaguer        )  Year: 2002
                              )
3              v.             )  Award Status:
4       Sportsmanship         )  Dishonorable Mention
5   _____   )
```

STRIKE ONE, YOU'RE OUT?

Jason Abbitt, 15, signed up with the Vallejo (California) Babe Ruth Baseball League. But Jason didn't get to play as much as he thought he should. "It got tiring," he said. "I just sat there. During the season, you had to dig a hole to find my self-esteem, it was so low." He said the previous year he "played less than 10 percent of the games. At the end of the year, [the coach] promised I'd be a starting player."

Hoping for improvement, he signed up again. But, he said, he only played "maybe 20 percent of the total innings." Then again, when he did get to play, he didn't like the position he was assigned. "I would like to have played second base, but when I did play, [the coach] stuck me out in right field because nothing gets hit out there." Double the play time wasn't good enough for Jason, who batted just .083 his second year, versus the best hitter's .368—he figured he sat on the bench during 80 percent of the games. "That's why I'm suing for 80 percent of the sign-up fee."

That's right: Since Jason paid $85 to sign up, and figures he didn't play 80 percent of the time, he sued the league in small-claims court for about 80 percent of the sign-up fee he paid: $65 plus court costs.

League president Dennis Clemente said he long ago told Jason's father, David Abbitt, 47, that there is "no guarantee of your son playing a single minute." He also told the Abbitts that it was possible to get sign-up fees reimbursed by appealing to the league's board, which considers such requests on a case-by-case basis. But, he said, neither Jason nor his father ever even asked the board for a refund.

"The big picture is he's a kid and he has feelings," David Abbitt said. "He's not paying to sit the bench." He complained the coaches are too focused on winning. "At this age it's not about winning or losing; it's about having fun. About heading into adulthood. [But] the coaches tend to think it's always the seventh game of the World Series."

Clemente said that's not true—it's the kids who are definitely playing to win. "There's not many that just want to come out and play. Most want to win and they get upset when they don't win." And the parents also get upset when their kid's team doesn't win, he said. When they don't, "they want their son traded to a better team." David did try to get Jason traded, but the request was turned down.

David said youth baseball is "about heading into adulthood." But instead of even attempting to go through the regular channels to get a refund, Jason sued the Babe Ruth League. One wonders: Did David's father spend as much time helping him be a better ball player as he did on complaining and supporting his lawsuit? If he had, maybe he would have been good enough to play more. But that's not how things are done in the victim culture that's growing in America.

Alas, Solano County Small Claims Court sent David to the showers—it dismissed his suit—showing him that sportsmanlike conduct means being able to accept losing. Welcome to adulthood, kid.

Thanks to being filed in small-claims court, the suit only took six weeks from filing to dismissal.

Sources:

* "Father, Son File Suit Against Babe Ruth League," *Vallejo Times-Herald*, 19 October 2002
* "Lawsuit Wasn't Worth the Hassle," *Vallejo Times-Herald*, 17 November 2002

1	*	) Location: California
2	Poverty Pimp	) Year: 2002
3	v.	) Award Status:
4	Newspaper Columnist	) Dishonorable Mention
5		)

PIMP PLUCKED

Columnist Jill Stewart of the now-defunct Los Angeles–based *New Times L.A.* newspaper got a chuckle when former mayor Richard Riordan blamed "poverty pimps" for "sucking up money that does not trickle down to the poor."

When asked to identify who exactly he meant, Riordan went mute. So Stewart wrote a column in which she "revealed" the "leading poverty pimp in Los Angeles is Danny Bakewell, founder of the Brotherhood Crusade." She called Bakewell "a key race-baiter" who is "one of about 10 self-appointed 'spokesmen' for the supposed group known as the 'L.A. black community.'"

Stewart said when she found out the multimillionaire developer had sued her for libel, she "experienced a moment of mild euphoria, like eating expensive chocolate on vacation" and "marveled over what Bakewell could possibly present in court to prove that I had libeled him by calling him a 'poverty pimp.'"

In her response to the suit, Stewart's defense was that Bakewell is a "poverty pimp" because he "recklessly manipulates racial divisions" and "preys upon the worst conspiratorial delusions of African-Americans for his own political gain" and then "leverages that political power for personal enrichment," which makes him "worse than Al Sharpton."

Superior Court Judge John P. Shook apparently liked the argument. He not only threw the suit out, he ordered Bakewell pay the *New Times* $25,000 in legal fees. Bakewell quickly settled for $20,000—which, the *New Times* reported, he paid with money from one of the charities he runs.

Source:

∗ "Pimped but Good," *New Times L.A.*, 29 August 2002

```
1                    *              )    Location: Illinois
2           Baseball Team          )    Year: 2002
                                   )
3                  v.              )    Award Status:
4        Stadium Neighbors         )    Dishonorable Mention
                                   )
5    ---------------------------------  )
```

AMERICA'S OTHER FAVORITE PASTIME

The Chicago Cubs baseball team was upset with the owners of bars around Wrigley Field, the park where the team plays home games. The team said the several businesses surrounding the stadium "unjustly enrich themselves" by letting customers sit on the bars' private properties.

Ummmm . . . *huh*? Team management said by letting people watch the games over the stadium walls from private buildings surrounding the park, the bars are stealing the team's "product" by violating its copyright on the games.

"You have [something] that has evolved from Weber grills and lawn chairs into a multimillion-dollar business by pirating our product," claimed Cubs President Andy MacPhail. The team filed a lawsuit in U.S. District Court against a group of bars after talks with the bar owners broke down. "They do nothing to contribute to our efforts to put a winning team on the field," he said. "The free ride is over."

The suit says the bars, which charge as much as $100 to $200 to watch a game from their rooftops, represent themselves as "small-time friends of the common fan . . . [but] are in fact free-riders who profiteer on plaintiff's enormous annual expenditures on, and historical investment in, the Chicago Cubs baseball team and Wrigley Field."

What do "enormous annual expenditures" have to do with anything? "During the 2002 season, the Cubs spent nearly $80 million on the salaries of the players on its major league roster," the suit says. "The Cubs pay millions of additional dollars annually to operate and maintain Wrigley Field, incur the team's travel and road trip costs and pay all of the other expenses of operating a team in Major League Baseball." Thus, the team contends, it has a right to control the view from private property. To bolster the copyright claim, the club contends the rooftop seating areas illegally provide TV sets so the faraway viewers can look at game broadcasts.

Well, which is it? Are the bars violating copyright by letting people look over the wall, or by letting them watch TV because the park is too far away?

Whatever. The suit seeks unspecified monetary damages and a court order prohibiting anyone with a private view of Wrigley Field from charging admission to view games at the park. The lawsuit came after the team rejected an offer from the bars to pay the Cubs $14 per patron, but only if it was called a "marketing fee" and not a license to watch the games.

In the old days, baseball was known as "America's Pastime." How fitting it's so intimately involved with America's new pastime: dragging every silly argument into court.

Sources:

* "Cubs Sue Owners of Rooftop Bars Overlooking Wrigley,"
  Associated Press, 17 December 2002
* "Cubs Hurl Federal Suit at Rooftop Owners," *Chicago Trib-
  une,* 17 December 2002

Afterword:

The bars settled the claim by agreeing to pay the baseball club $15 to $25 for each patron. The Cubs claimed
that as many as seventeen hundred patrons were watching the games from bar rooftops, so the settlement is expected to net the team $1.2 million to $1.7 million a year.
Three of the bar owners, however, refused to participate in
the settlement agreement. "We are completely confident in
our position," said their lawyer, Chris Gair. "The Cubs
don't own the view from our buildings. We own the view
from our buildings." The legal case was pending for just
over a year.

Source:

* "Rooftop Owners Agree to Pay Cubs," *Chicago Sun-Times,*
  January 11, 2004

Chicago: A Lawyer's Kind of Town

In 2001 and 2002, the city of Chicago paid out a total of $98 million in lawsuit judgments and settlements. That includes $99,000 in a class-action case to five thousand panhandlers (which amounts to an average of $19.80 each)—while the lawyers who handled the case received $375,000 in fees. But don't feel bad if you're a resident of Chicago: New York spends $550 million per year on lawsuits.

(*Source: Newsweek*)

```
1              *           )   Location: California
                           )
2        Grieving Mother   )   Year: 2002
                           )
3              v.          )   Award Status:
                           )   Dishonorable Mention
4            Bridge        )
                           )
5    ----------------------)
```

JUMPING ON THE BANDWAGON

Cases of suicide can be tragic, especially when there is a juvenile involved. But must a suicide be a reason to find someone to blame?

Marissa Imrie, 14, of Santa Rosa, California, hired a cab for a $150 ride to San Francisco's Golden Gate Bridge. She had the cabbie let her off at the south end of the bridge, a popular tourist spot at the end of a sidewalk where people can stroll across the span. The last time the cabbie saw Imrie, she was heading up that sidewalk.

The Coast Guard pulled her body from the water later the same day. She had jumped off the bridge.

Imrie's mother, Renee Milligan, sued the Golden Gate Bridge, Highway and Transportation District, and its board of directors, saying the bridge authority should have built an "effective" suicide barrier on the bridge, as it is well known as the world's most popular suicide spot. She bases her claim on California's wrongful death statutes, and says the bridge creates a "dangerous condition on public property."

But such an argument is enough to put a jury to sleep.

If there's anything Americans know, it's that *they have rights*. But how do you jazz up a suicide case to make it a rights case?

The suit claims the lack of a suicide barrier is a violation of the dead girl's Constitutional right not to be deprived of life without due process of law. As long as we're stretching that far, the lawyers must have thought, they threw in more: The girl's death *also* infringes on the *mother's* rights, too! The suit argues that Milligan's "constitutional right of familial association" was violated.

The suit asks for a court order forcing the bridge board to erect a suicide barrier and pay Milligan various unspecified actual and punitive financial damages.

If anyone has a "right to life"—and the corresponding right to end it—it's the person living it. Doesn't second-guessing that person's decision by suing take that right away?

Source:

* "Mother Sues GG Bridge District over Girl's Suicide," *Bay City News,* 17 December 2002

Afterword:

The trial court agreed with the Bridge District's motion for "demurrer" (a plea for dismissal on the grounds that even if the facts alleged in the complaint were true, there is no legal basis for a lawsuit). That ruling was appealed, but on June 4, 2004, the California Court of Appeal affirmed the decision. Elapsed time from suicide to appeal decision: about two and a half years.

Source:

* Court records

1	*	) Location: Kansas
2	The Accidentally	) Year: 2003
3	Offended	) Award Status:
4	v.	) Dishonorable Mention
5	Airline	)

NO RHYME OR REASON

When you were a child, did you use a rhyme to choose other kids for your team? It might have been, "Eenie, meenie, minie, moe; catch a tiger by the toe. . . ." If you're less than 50 years old, you might be surprised to hear that the rhyme's mid–nineteenth century roots are quite racist; that "tiger" line used to be commonly recited as "catch a nigger by the toe."

Southwest Airlines flight attendant Jennifer Cundiff, 22 at the time, was pretty surprised to find out—she had never heard the racist version. She had picked up a twist on the rhyme from other flight attendants and, on a crowded 2001 flight, got on the intercom to tell boarding passengers, "Eenie, meenie, minie, moe; pick a seat, we gotta go."

Two of those passengers were sisters Louise Sawyer, 46, and Grace Fuller, 48, both of whom are black. They sued Southwest, claiming they were discriminated against and suffered physical and emotional distress, and demanded unspecified actual and punitive damages, arguing that the young flight attendant used a known racist rhyme to specifically demean them.

U.S. District Court Judge Kathryn H. Vratil of Kansas City, Kansas, dismissed the distress claims, but ruled that the rest of the case could proceed to trial. "The court agrees with plaintiffs that because of its history, the phrase 'eenie, meenie, minie, moe' could reasonably be viewed as objectively racist and offensive," she wrote. "The jury, however, must decide whether Cundiff's remark was racist, or simply a benign and innocent attempt at humor," as well as find that the women were denied "the same enjoyment that others experienced on that flight."

Thanks to the passage of time, millions of people had never heard the "nigger" version of the rhyme, only the innocent one. By insisting that a 22-year-old *must* have been intentionally racist when any rational observer sees no racism only helps perpetuate the hurtful version of the rhyme. In their greed, Sawyer and Fuller have given a long-dead bit of racism new life.

Source:

* "Rhyme at Center of Lawsuit Against Southwest Airlines," *Kansas City Star,* 10 February 2003

Afterword:

After a two-day trial—and just one hour of deliberation— the jury ruled the two sisters did not suffer discrimination. After the ruling the women claimed they were discriminated against again—by the jury. "If we had jurors of our peers, then we would have won the case today," claimed plaintiff Grace Fuller, who said the flight attendant's re-mark caused her to have a seizure, leaving her bedridden for three days. The case took about three years from inci-dent to dismissal.

Source:

* "Jury Decides Rhyme Not Malicious," Associated Press, 22 January 2004

```
1              *              )   Location: Wisconsin
                              )
2        Proselytizer        )   Year: 2003
                              )
3             v.              )   Award Status:
                              )   Dishonorable Mention
4       The Unconverted       )
                              )
5   ----------------------------)
```

TAKE 'EM FOR A RIDE

Gail Anderson, 56, was riding the bus in Milwaukee, Wisconsin, and was on a mission: She was proselytizing her religion to other passengers, trying to press literature and *The Book of Hope* Bibles on them.

When the driver asked her to stop, she refused. The driver again asked her to stop, telling her that county rules prohibited the distribution of "any form of advertising or literature" on the transit system. She again refused and was "escorted" off the bus.

Anderson filed a federal suit in Milwaukee's U.S. District Court claiming violation of her rights to free speech and freedom of religion against the Milwaukee County Department of Public Works, the DPW's transit division, and Milwaukee Transport Services, Inc., which operates the county transit system. She has asked the court to declare the county rule invalid and award her unspecified damages.

"Forcefully removing Ms. Anderson from the bus because she distributed the Bible was a humiliating experience," claimed her attorney, Mathew D. Staver. "Passengers don't shed their constitutional rights when they enter public transportation venues."

Freedom of speech is a primary right in the United States, but since when did it include the right to force others to listen? By insinuating herself upon a captive audience, she ignored the responsibilities that go hand in hand with her rights. The answer to "What Would Jesus Do?" is not, "File a lawsuit!"

Source:

* "Bible Donor Sues after Driver Kicks Her Off Bus," *Milwaukee Journal Sentinel,* 10 June 2003

```
1                    *           )   Location: New York
                                 )
2              Bus Driver        )   Year: 2003
                                 )
3                 v.             )   Award Status:
                                 )   Dishonorable Mention
4          Employee Manual       )
                                 )
5   --------------------------------
```

RED LIGHT /
GREEN LIGHT / WHO
CAN I / SUE TONIGHT?

Curtis Shannon was a bus driver for the New York City Transit Authority. About six weeks after starting his job he was involved in a minor accident. Part of the Authority's normal post-accident procedure required Shannon to get a medical clearance to go back to work, but he failed his eye exam—he was found to be red-green color-blind, and unable to distinguish traffic light colors.

Shannon was given an exhaustive series of follow-up tests by several different doctors, including two consulting ophthalmologists not employed by the NYCTA, who confirmed his inability to see color correctly.

Federal law requires that commercial drivers be able to correctly discern the colors in traffic lights. Shannon was thus given a choice: Resign his position or be fired. He resigned, but filed a complaint with the Equal Employment Opportunity Commission claiming that he was not given "reasonable accommodation" to do his job per the Americans with Disabilities Act—even though he denies being color-blind. He also filed suit against the NYCTA claiming discrimination on the basis of the "disability" he denied having.

When the court threw out the suit, Shannon appealed to the U.S. Court of Appeals. The appeals court agreed with NYCTA policy—and U.S. Department of Transportation rules for commercial drivers—that a bus driver being able to properly distinguish the color of traffic lights is an "essential function" of his job, and that a "reasonable accommodation can never involve the elimination of an essential function of a job."

The court also ruled that the lower court's finding that Shannon could not distinguish the different colors of traffic lights was reasonable, considering the testimony of several different doctors, and upheld the dismissal of Shannon's case—to the considerable relief of every pedestrian, driver, and bus passenger in the city.

Source:

* Decision of the U.S. Court of Appeals for the Second District, Docket 02-7266, 13 June 2003

Medical "Insurance"

According to *Newsweek* magazine, U.S. doctors order up between $50 billion and $100 billion of unneeded tests, consultations, and other "defensive medicine" to protect themselves against lawsuits—which is enough to provide medical insurance to all of the estimated forty million Americans who have none. Worse, the magazine points out, studies show that the vast majority of medical malpractice cases don't result in lawsuits, while about 80 percent of medical malpractice cases that are filed are bogus.

```
1              *          )  Location: Illinois
2      Movie Villains     )  Year: 2003
                          )
3           v.            )  Award Status:
4      Movie Producer     )  Dishonorable Mention
                          )
5                         )
```

CAT FIGHT

"Ah-ahhhhhh-ah-*ahhhhhhhhhhhrrrrrgh*!" may be the new refrain of "George of the Jungle" after one corporate behemoth went after another. The Walt Disney Company's direct-to-video movie *George of the Jungle 2* stirred the wrath of Caterpillar, Inc., makers of bulldozers and other industrial equipment.

It seems the plotline of *GJ2* has to do with a bad-guy industrialist trying to level the jungle where George lives. The climax is a several-minute sequence in which George fights off the evil environment-destroying "bulldozing bullies" who are, you guessed it, driving Caterpillar-brand dozers. And the company doesn't like that. It doesn't like that one bit.

So much so that Caterpillar sued Disney and Buena Vista Entertainment, its distribution subsidiary, asking the U.S. District Court in Peoria, Illinois, to stop the movie's distribution and force Disney to recall the 2.2 million copies that had already been distributed so they could edit out the disparaging scenes. The basis? Trademark dilution and infringement. They say the movie's use of Cat-branded equipment "ties" Caterpillar to an "evil attacking army," which might create a "negative impact on children that view the movie."

Yeah. That could happen. Sure.

It's true that the owners of registered trademarks must diligently go after those who infringe on their rights or they can lose the trademark. The makers of Kleenex-brand facial tissues are fighting that right now, trying to keep the word "Kleenex" from becoming a generic word. That's what happened to "thermos" already. But certainly Disney is not going to branch into heavy equipment and compete with Cat, and the profits from the movie don't depend on the brand of dozer shown.

Taking Cat's argument to its extreme, if a bad guy drives a Lincoln Town Car in a movie, Lincoln Mercury should sue and whine that having a fictional criminal drive its cars somehow puts the company in a bad light. Maybe Cat thinks big industrialists like to watch stupid video movies and are somehow dumb enough to think that because some fictional characters use a particular brand of equipment, it means they shouldn't buy that brand? Is that what they really want their customers to think of them, that they're unthinking morons? Nice marketing ploy, guys!

"While we have great respect for Caterpillar, we consider this without legal merit," Disney said in a statement in response to the suit. "We expect the audience will view these sequences for their comedic value and not take them seriously." Otherwise known as the application of common sense and the consideration of a reasonable interpretation of the context by ordinary people.

U.S. District Court Judge Joe McDade agreed with that concept. He was unimpressed with Cat's arguments and refused to issue the preliminary injunctions the company asked for. McDade said there was no evidence that Disney was attempting to "somehow poach or free-ride" on Caterpillar's trademarks to increase the movie's sales. He doubted that the use of the logo on the machines in the movie would make anyone think the company supported or endorsed the film, and the appearance of well-known trademarks in movies or TV shows was indeed a "common phenomenon."

Caterpillar said they'd study the ruling before deciding what to do next. Stella's suggestion: Quit acting like the big mean company you're accusing Disney of making you look like!

Meanwhile, toy manufacturer Wham-O of Hula Hoop and Frisbee fame is also steaming mad at a movie: *Dickie Roberts: Former Child Star,* starring David Spade. In the film, Spade tosses a Slip 'n' Slide on his lawn, coats it with oil, and jumps on. He slides past the end and crashes into a fence. An obvious comedy bit, sure, but that's way too much for Wham-O.

The toy company filed suit against Paramount Pictures and Happy Madison Productions contending the film (yep!) infringes its trademark. It asks the court to order Paramount to pull the film from theaters and either remove the scene or add a disclaimer that people ought not to try that at home. They say the scene violates the toy's "safety guidelines," which among other things say the toy should only be used by children aged 5 through 12 weighing less than 110 pounds and under five feet tall—which, come to think of it, sounds very suspiciously like a description of David Spade.

Sources:

* "George of the Jungle, Watch Out for That Lawsuit!" Reuters, 15 October 2003
* "Caterpillar Sues to Block Release of Disney Movie," Associated Press, 15 October 2003
* "Judge Refuses Caterpillar Request to Block Disney Release," Associated Press, 20 October 2003
* "Slip 'n' Slide Makers Sue 'Dickie Roberts'," Associated Press, 8 September 2003

Afterword:

Quite a few readers defended the case against Disney. One argued: "I'm rather surprised at your attitude toward this action by Caterpillar unless you are unaware of Disney's practice of prosecuting copyright infringement. If someone else used a Disney character in one of their movies I feel safe in assuming Disney's attorneys would be hot on their case to have it removed. Caterpillar is doing no less than this. It would have been easy to have used a generic type of earth-moving equipment in this cartoon, as has been done in others."

Trademark and copyright are both "intellectual property," but they are vastly different concepts. While I'd welcome a case submission of Disney filing a frivolous suit, I'm not aware of any recent ones, and my call for readers to bring any to my attention brought silence. Even if they have recently pressed such a suit, that has nothing to do with how frivolous Cat's suit is: Two wrongs don't make a right.

It Ought to Be a Crime
Lawsuits by Inmates and Criminals

Some prison inmates serving time are harming their victims again: by suing them. Or suing the prison, or the state, or their own attorneys, or anyone else they can think of. And, unfortunately, they have all the time they need to think about their case. Sometimes, if the criminals themselves can't pursue their case, family members are ready to fill in for them to collect a few bucks from the victims.

```
1              *         )   Location: California
                         )
2           Felon        )   Year: 2003
                         )
3            v.          )   Award Status:
                         )   Dishonorable Mention
4         His Victim     )
                         )
5   -------------------- )
```

SHAGGY DOG STORY

In February 2000, Sara McBurnett bumped into an SUV on a freeway on-ramp in San Jose, California. The driver of the SUV came to her window, and she rolled it down to apologize to him. But the enraged man reached into her car, grabbed her pet dog Leo from her lap, and threw the animal into freeway traffic, where it was run over and killed as McBurnett watched in horror.

The man fled, and his cruel actions sparked international headlines—and a manhunt. Private donations poured in, totaling more than $100,000 in rewards to help catch the road-rager. Andrew Burnett, 27, was eventually identified as the man in the SUV; he was convicted of felony animal cruelty and, in July 2001, given the maximum sentence: three years in prison.

Less than two years later, from his cell, Burnett found a way to make his rage reach back out into the real world once again. He filed a lawsuit claiming McBurnett slandered him in her statements to the police and the *San Jose Mercury News* newspaper, and claimed that the newspaper libeled him by "knowingly and maliciously" printing those "defamatory" remarks that, he claims, created the international furor over what he did that rainy night. That, he says in the suit he filed without an attorney, caused him "mental pain and anguish, humiliation, embarrassment, fright and shock, and mortification," plus post-traumatic stress disorder and loss of wages. For all that, Burnett demands more than $1 million in compensation from McBurnett and the newspaper.

By abusing the civil courts, violent criminals no longer have to be satisfied with causing mental pain, anguish, fright, shock, and mortification while they're loose on the streets, since once they're imprisoned they have all the time in the world to do it all over again—by suing their victims for reporting their crime or for some other made-up slight. Crime victims are fearful enough; convicted criminals must lose the right to sue their victims, or society will suffer when victims begin to think twice about reporting crimes to the authorities.

Source:

* "Leo the Dog's Killer Claims Mental Anguish in Suit," *San Jose Mercury News,* 28 February 2003

```
1                    *              )  Location: Utah
                                    )
2        Wanna-be Vampire          )  Year: 2002
                                    )
3               v.                  )  Award Status: Runner-up
                                    )  for the 2002 Stella Award
4             Prison               )
                                    )
5  ---------------------------------)
```

I VANT TO SUCK
YOUR VALLET

Robert Paul Rice, an inmate in Utah serving one to fifteen years on weapons, theft, and burglary convictions, sued the Utah Department of Corrections claiming his prison was not letting him practice his religion.

Well, that certainly sounds serious! How dare they? But hold on: Rice says he's a Druid Vampire, and must be allowed sexual access to a "vampress" and partake "in the vampiric sacrament"—drinking blood.

Rice claimed that he had told the prison he was a Druid, and "the order of the Druids that I follow is the order of the Vampire" with specific "vampiric dietary needs," but his records show that he registered as a Catholic when he was imprisoned in 2000.

When Judge J. Dennis Frederick dismissed his suit, Rice appealed. The Utah Court of Appeals upheld the dismissal, noting that the suit "raises questions that are so insubstantial as not to merit further consideration."

As for the sexual favors of any female vampires, "Without any question we do not have conjugal visits in Utah," says a prison spokesman. Proving once again that prison life sucks.

Sources:

* "Self-styled 'Vampire' Prisoner Denied Conjugal Visits," Associated Press, 26 October 2002
* "Rice v. Department of Corrections," Utah Court of Appeals, Case No. 20020451-CA, 24 October 2002

```
1              *              )  Location: New York
                              )
2        Bill Skipper         )  Year: 2004
                              )
3            v.               )  Award Status:
                              )  Dishonorable Mention
4       Her Credit Card       )
                              )
5    ------------------------
```

JUST CHARGE IT

Police in New York say Antoinette Millard, 40, a former vice president at the Brown Brothers Harriman
investment bank, posed as a Saudi Arabian princess and
as a Victoria's Secret fashion model, and fraudulently stole
hundreds of thousands of dollars' worth of merchandise.
Millard is not Saudi Arabian, nor has she ever been a Victoria's Secret model; she's from a "blue-collar family" in
Buffalo.

One of those allegedly conned was American Express,
which had issued her a coveted "Black" AmEx card, which
she used to run up huge bills. She was arrested and
charged with grand larceny, and was freed after posting
$100,000 bail. She has also been charged with insurance
fraud after allegedly filing a false $262,000 insurance
claim for jewelry she claimed had been stolen but prosecutors say she really sold.

American Express sued Millard for payment of her
$951,000 outstanding charge card balance.

But Millard insists she's not liable for the payments,
since American Express "induced" her to sign up for the
no-credit-limit card, and promised she could make "flexible payments" on her balance. In a countersuit, she blames

the company for its "false and fraudulent" promises since "in truth and in fact [American Express] did not allow [Millard] to make flexible payments." Further, the suit says, Millard "was suffering from anorexia, depression, panic attacks, head tumors and by reason of such illnesses was mentally incompetent and unable of executing or making any agreement as alleged" in the suit filed by American Express.

AmEx, meanwhile, "knew or should have known that [Millard] was acting impulsively and irrationally at the time she entered into contract," and thus AmEx should pay *her* $2 million.

"She's someone who got caught up in the money culture that dominates New York, and the need to fit in with that culture," said her lawyer, Peter Brill. When asked if Millard had a psychological problem, he replied, "I think everybody in New York has a long-standing psychological problem."

No doubt Brill is from New York. Draw your own conclusions.

Sources:

* "Fake Saudi Princess-Model Countersues American Express," Associated Press, 24 November 2004
* "Lessons in Human Buy-ology," *San Francisco Chronicle*, 19 December 2004

```
1              *              )  Location: Ohio
2         Burglar             )  Year: 2004
3            v.               )  Award Status:
4         Police              )  Dishonorable Mention
5  _____     )
```

WITHOUT REMORSE

Police officers investigating a hot burglary in Akron, Ohio, found the suspect hiding in a cabinet. They said Christopher Sample, 27, initially showed his hands to the officers and was surrendering, but then suddenly pulled his hands back and shoved them into his coat.

The closest officer, fearing Sample had a gun in his coat, opened fire, hitting Sample several times in the arms and legs. When they searched him, however, they did not find a gun.

Sample pleaded guilty to burglary and served six months in prison for the break-in.

The officer-involved shooting was investigated by the police department and local prosecutors and was deemed justified. "We are 100 percent sure that the officer acted appropriately," said Paul Hlynsky, president of the local Fraternal Order of Police union. "He went through an intense investigation and his conduct was flawless." No charges were filed against the officer.

But that, of course, only covers criminal charges. Now that he is out of prison, Sample has filed a civil lawsuit in the Summit County Common Pleas Court against Officer Jason Bailey, the Akron Police Department, and the city of

Akron, claiming that Bailey shot him "without warning, explanation or provocation." The suit claims that his wounds have kept him from getting work since he got out of prison, and he wants to be reimbursed for $45,000 in medical expenses. The suit seeks unspecified further damages.

Perhaps a better explanation for why Sample can't get work is that potential employers who hear his background consider him dangerous. And rightly so. When confronted by armed police officers while committing crimes, felons should realize the jig is up and do exactly what they're told, such as, "FREEZE!" Making threatening moves against a man pointing a gun at you isn't "unprovoked," it's begging for a sucking chest wound.

Felons lose many of their civil rights when they commit their crimes. Yet criminals, either freshly out of prison or even still incarcerated, retain the right to sue the police— or even their victims—greatly increasing the burden they place on society and the toll on their victims. Felons simply should not have the right to sue their victims or the police officers who capture them unless they can first prove that a crime has been committed against them, such as the use of unreasonable force. When, for instance, a police officer is completely exonerated by an outside agency for shooting a felon, that should be the end of the story unless a higher police authority (such as the state police) finds criminal conduct.

Criminals made the choice to be where they don't belong and do things they knew they shouldn't be doing. Any injuries sustained in the pursuit of criminal activities are their own fault, and there should be no recourse for them in the civil courts. By definition, they have chosen not to abide by the rules of society; why should they be allowed to turn around and choose to use those very same rules against their victims just because it suddenly suits them?

Meanwhile, it's not particularly surprising that Sample is in trouble again: After filing his suit he was arrested on charges of felony vandalism and misdemeanor resisting arrest. Clearly, even being shot when resisting arrest wasn't a good enough lesson to keep him from doing it again.

Source:

* "Burglar Suing Officer Who Shot Him," *Akron Beacon Journal,* 16 January 2004

(In)Hospitable Venues

The Harris Poll interviewed 1,437 senior corporate attorneys about the lawsuit climate in the country and their states. Sixty percent gave an overall ranking of "fair" or "poor" to the state court liability system in the U.S. in 2005, compared to 54 percent the year before. The attorneys were asked to grade the states in ten areas: tort and contract litigation, treatment of class-action suits, punitive damages, timeliness of summary judgment or dismissal, discovery, scientific and technical evidence, the competence of judges, the impartiality of judges, jury competence, and jury fairness. The states with the best grades were Delaware, Nebraska, North Dakota, Virginia, and Iowa. The bottom five were Illinois, Louisiana, Alabama, West Virginia, and Mississippi. Mississippi was dead last in nine of the ten areas studied; it also came in last in 2004, 2003, and 2002. (*Source: Harris Interactive, commissioned by the U.S. Chamber Institute for Legal Reform*)

```
1              *              )   Location: Pennsylvania
2      Burglar's Family       )   Year: 2002
3              v.             )   Award Status:
4         His Victim          )   Dishonorable Mention
5                             )
```

DEAD BURGLAR GETS TO KEEP THE LOOT

In 1994, Frank Lucisano thought he heard someone breaking into a shed behind his Tullytown, Pennsylvania, home. He grabbed his shotgun and confronted the burglar: Howard Reid, 29.

A scuffle broke out and Lucisano shot Reid, killing him. District Attorney Alan Rubenstein declared the shooting justified—after all, Lucisano was physically attacked by a man committing a felony. In fact, Rubenstein said at the time, "If you want to deter burglars, an occasional shooting may have a wonderful effect."

But that didn't stop the burglar's mother, Dorothy Reid, from suing Lucisano in 1996, claiming her son was shot "without provocation"—despite the D.A.'s findings. After years of legal wrangling, both sides agreed to binding arbitration. The arbitrator, attorney Barbara Lyons, held that the shooting was a "purposeful deed" and awarded the burglar's family $50,000.

If you want to encourage burglars, there's nothing like the ability to sue if the victim catches you in the act. Why submit to lawful arrest when you can get big money if you attack your victim instead?

Crime has always been a "high-risk" occupation. Is it really in society's best interests to reduce that risk, thus encouraging more crime?

Even though the case was heard by arbitration (with an attorney as the arbitrator), the elapsed time from incident to resolution still took eight years.

Source:

* "Burglar's Family Awarded $50,000," *Bucks County Courier Times,* 13 October 2002

```
1                  *            )  Location: South Carolina
2       Criminal's Family       )  Year: 2003
                                )
3              v.               )  Award Status:
4     Pretty Much Everyone      )  Dishonorable Mention
5   --------------------------  )
```

PURSUING A DEEP POCKET

Police in Clemson, South Carolina, received a report that a man in a vehicle had tried to run down a pedestrian near an apartment building. When officers arrived, they spotted Ron Brown, 23, racing away from the scene. They gave chase, but Brown refused to pull over.

With police hot on his tail during the four A.M. pursuit, Brown drove into a construction area—and drove off the end of a bridge under construction. He was killed in the resulting crash. No police car ever hit him: He crashed completely from his own actions after choosing his own escape path.

But his father, Bob Brown, has filed a wrongful death suit against:

* The City of Clemson, whose police chased his son and "forced" him to drive into a "dangerous construction zone."

* The Thrift Brothers Construction Company, which did not anticipate the need to have sufficient signs and barriers

to stop a crazed man who was fleeing the police at high
speed.

* The South Carolina Department of Transportation, for
  failing to properly "inspect and supervise" the construction company working on the highway bridge.

* The apartment complex where the chase started.

* The apartment complex employee who called the police
  in the first place.

So there's a great way to set public policy: Anyone who
sees a potential crime occurring, say, someone trying to
run a pedestrian down, shouldn't call the police to report
it because they might be sued for appealing for help?

The father's suit asks for unspecified "actual and punitive damages." By running from the police, Ron was trying to escape responsibility for his own actions. Gee . . .
where do you suppose he learned a lesson like that?

Source:

* "Clemson, State DOT Are Sued: Father Files Lawsuit over
  Son's Deadly Police Chase," *Anderson Independent-Mail*,
  1 October 2002

The Class-Action Lottery
The Queue Forms Here

Sometimes it is alleged that a company or its products harmed many people—a "class" of consumers. Often the allegations are true, but sometimes it's more like a lottery, with plaintiffs piling on in hopes of securing a windfall when their number comes up, whether or not they were actually damaged by the product.

Then there's the *real* reason class-action suits are so popular: When you follow the money, the motivation becomes obvious. The "class" rarely gets much of anything, but the lawyers clean up, collecting millions of dollars in fees. When it's all over, they look for another victim with deep pockets. Lather, rinse, repeat.

1	*)	Location: Massachusetts
2	Nitpickers)	Year: 2003
3	v.)	Award Status:
4	Every Store in the State)	Dishonorable Mention
5	)	

FORGET THE PRICE, WHAT'S THE COST?

The state of Massachusetts still has on its books a law requiring stores to individually mark each item for sale with the price. In an era of bar code scanners and automated checkout (and even bar code readers scattered through stores for shoppers to use if they forget what the shelf card said), Massachusetts still wants every can, lightbulb, and package of screws offered for sale to be marked with a price.

Naturally, most stores ignore the outdated law. Similar laws have long been repealed in most states, and for good reason: People want low prices, and it's expensive to mark prices on every tiny item, especially if it goes on sale once in a while. Consumers are damaged, too: If price changes are costly for merchants, they're not encouraged to compete on price.

The law predates computerized checkout, but Colman Herman, 59, doesn't care—the law's the law, he says. The Dorchester, Massachusetts, resident complained to Home Depot because the thirty-three stores it runs in the state didn't mark prices on items—just as most stores don't. They refused to do anything. He complained to the state attorney general, who also refused to enforce the state law; obviously he didn't consider it much of an issue.

But Herman didn't back down. He sued, even gaining class-action status to represent all consumers who were "victimized" by Home Depot's refusal to put a price sticker on every light switch and piece of lumber. The suit asked for $25 "for each consumer affected" by Home Depot's actions. No doubt the word "affected" was used since they couldn't really say "harmed" with a straight face.

Home Depot, knowing the law was clearly not on its side, settled, offering $3.8 million. In addition, it agreed to get its thirty-three stores into compliance with the state pricing law within three years, an effort which it estimates will cost $20 million.

Of that $3.8 million settlement, half will go to Herman's attorneys. The rest will be divided up among an "eclectic" mix of consumer groups and charities—and the Massachusetts attorney general, the very one who determined that going after Home Depot in the first place was not a good use of government funds. The major beneficiaries didn't even have to show if they were harmed, let alone how. They include Habitat for Humanity ($1 million); the National Consumer Law Center ($100,000); the Friends of the Shattuck Shelter ($50,000); a "consumer advocate" Web site registered to an individual, not a nonprofit organization ($25,000); and a new entity called the "Consumer Resource Fund" ($725,000), from which the attorney general will get an unspecified share.

Note that none of the money will go to Colman Herman, even though he's listed as the "lead plaintiff," nor to any other members of the "class" (you know, the "victims" that were "affected" by Home Depot's actions). Why not? Well, the *Boston Globe* reports, "apparently because the damages per person are so small"—at least, once all the nonaffected groups and the attorneys grab their shares, there's so little left that it would cost too much to find the individual members of the class. Maybe that's why Home Depot settled before going to trial: They were probably afraid of a jury ordering them to mail checks for a penny each to five hundred thousand people.

Home Depot was literally so grateful the Suffolk Superior Court accepted its settlement offer, its spokesman said the outcome was "the best possible outcome under the circumstances." The spokesman refused to comment on whether the law was reasonable. "The bottom line is it's the law and whether it's good or bad it is the law, and we are bound to comply with it."

Home Depot did not admit to any wrongdoing, and said in its settlement agreement that it believed "few, if any" consumers were injured by its actions. Still, coughing up nearly $24 million—which cost will, of course, be passed on to consumers in the form of higher prices—was "the best possible outcome" it could think of. It not only got to make forced "donations" to lawyers and housing and consumer groups, it found it politic to express gratitude over the extortion.

Other state retailers are outraged that Home Depot settled rather than fight the law. "This could have an impact right on down to the corner hardware store," complained president Jon Hurst of the Retail Association of Massachusetts. "If [Herman]'s promoting himself as a consumer advocate, I think he's pretty mixed up"—the costs borne by Home Depot and several other retailers "targeted" by such suits will be passed on to consumers, he said, adding his organization will renew its efforts to get the state law repealed.

Why does Herman fight against big companies for virtually no reward? "It's fun," he said.

Meanwhile, after earning his lawyers $1.9 million and nothing for himself, Herman is gearing up for a price tag sequel: He has filed an action against Wal-Mart.

Sources:

* "$3.8m Accord on Pricing," *Boston Globe,* 19 November 2002
* "Item-Pricing Crusader Takes on Wal-Mart," *Boston Globe,* 6 October 2002

Tort Costs: Out of Control?

A comparison of the U.S. civil litigation system to other types of compensation systems is quite telling. In 2002, approximately $233 billion was awarded in lawsuits, and 54 percent was paid to "expenses" relating to collecting that total (mostly attorney fees). Yet the same year, the "no fault" workers' compensation insurance system only cost 17 percent of the total compensation paid, even though there are often lawyers involved. In contrast, the expense ratio for Social Security benefits was only about 3 percent.

(*Source: Swiss Re*)

```
1            *            )  Location: Nationwide
2      A Slight Cough     )  Year: 2003
3            v.            )  Award Status:
4   Every Industry That   )  Dishonorable Mention
5       Ever Existed      )
                          )
```

IT'S BETTER THAN
THE LOTTERY

Asbestos is a natural insulating material that was commonly used in industry and buildings. It resists even open flames. Its amazing properties have been known so long that the very word "asbestos" is from the ancient Greek (for "inextinguishable or indestructible"). The Romans used asbestos as wicks for lamps since it didn't burn. It came into heavy use in the United States thanks to the railroads—it insulated the boilers in steam locomotives, helping make the job of keeping the engines running from resembling toiling in hell.

During World War II, shipyards used plenty of it, and studies later found that 1.4 percent of dockworkers later died from lung diseases. By the 1960s, it was widely realized that airborne asbestos fibers could cause severe lung problems, including lung cancer or mesothelioma, a deadly cancer of the lung, heart, or abdominal lining. Manufacturers started a massive switch-over to other insulating products such as fiberglass and cellulose.

Ahhhhh . . . did you say personal injury? Did you say

big pockets (er . . . industry)? "Step right up!" beg ads run all over the country in magazines and newspapers, on TV and radio—ads placed by lawyers looking to cash in on the asbestos lawsuit craze by finding someone, anyone, who might have been exposed to asbestos so they can sue. Currently there are more than three hundred thousand asbestos-related lawsuits pending. Insurance industry studies show that around 80 percent of the people suing have no symptoms or other signs of any disease caused by asbestos, yet about seventy thousand more cases are being filed every year. About seven hundred law firms are actively seeking clients for asbestos-related lawsuits, many using "mobile clinics" to "screen" otherwise healthy people by scouring medical histories or even taking X-rays in the search for any evidence that they may be a "victim."

At one screening location in Hazelwood, Missouri, visited by newspaper reporters, nineteen people were standing in line. Three said they had previously worked with asbestos and were there to get a free checkup. The sixteen others simply admitted they thought it could be a good way to make some quick money.

A nearly retired Boeing worker was getting a chest X-ray to look for a "shadow" in his lungs. "The lawyers said I could get $10,000 or $12,000 if the shadow is big enough," he said. A legacy for his children if he dies early? Nope: "I know just the fishing boat I'd buy with that." Had he ever worked with asbestos? "No, but lawyers say it's all over the place, so I was probably exposed to it." (If the lawyers acknowledge it was "all over the place," then how do they know any health damage was caused by his employer? Ah, well, that's just a slightly inconvenient detail.)

Another man who worked at a Ford plant "saw the notice in the union newsletter and figured 'Why not?'" he said. "It's better than the lottery. If they find something, I get a few thousand dollars I didn't have. If they don't find anything, I've just lost an afternoon." During his interview he chain-smoked cigarettes.

"We're here because the president of the retirees club called us and asked if we'd set up the screening," said Randy Gori, an attorney with one of the trolling law firms. "We're doing it as a favor," he said.

"He said what?" demanded Claude Barnes, the president of Local 837 of the International Association of Machinists and Aerospace Workers Union, when he heard about the "favor" claim. "Hell, they called me a half-dozen times to let them set this up. I didn't think it could do any harm and maybe some of the guys would get a little money. But it was the lawyers who wanted to do this." Gee, would lawyers actually lie just to get their hands on huge pots of money, even at the risk of bankrupting the companies that employ their clients? On the other hand, they probably don't want you to consider that question. . . .

Promising to sue "anyone who made products with asbestos who hasn't gone bankrupt yet," Martin Mengarelli, Gori's partner in the screening, said two screenings done earlier in the year found that half of the six hundred men and women tested "came back positive for asbestos-related disease," which doesn't actually mean they have any illness, or will ever suffer any ill effects.

Larry Sartin, the national director for occupational disease programs for the Paper, Allied-Industrial, Chemical & Energy Workers Union, said one law firm alone screened more than ten thousand possibly exposed workers in 2001. "We used to get settlement[s] pretty quick," he said, "but now with twenty-five or so companies bankrupt, it can take three or four years" to find a company with both some sort of liability and some amount of money or insurance.

Despite the heavy caseload, the screenings have actually slowed down recently because so many companies who used asbestos have filed for bankruptcy. They include Johns Manville, W. R. Grace, Federal Mogul, Pittsburgh Corning and U.S. Gypsum. Lawyers are now looking toward "second tier" companies—smaller manufacturers who haven't gone bankrupt yet.

So the fishing for victims is far from over. "I was tested positive and I haven't felt bad," said Union president Barnes. "I don't have a breathing problem." Yet he has already received two settlement checks for a total of $600— all that was left after the attorneys took their cut, which is typically one-quarter to one-half the payment. He said he doesn't know how much he'll get over time, but "I'm guessing a few thousand dollars if I'm lucky."

And he's only one of three thousand people lining up at the rapidly draining cash trough.

In exchange for the mere hundreds or even several thousands of dollars of settlement payments, Barnes and others have given up the right to sue—even if they get lung cancer or mesothelioma, which can cost $300,000 to $500,000 to treat. "We're gambling that we never get sick," Barnes said. "We were gambling when we took that test."

"Critics of screening say law firms do it just to bring in business," said Will Miller, a partner of the law firm that ran the Hazelwood screenings. "In reality, that may be correct." So obviously not all the lawyers in this business lie. Then he quickly added, "But people are often helped by the results of the screenings." (Remember: Lawyers do such screenings as a "favor.") He said in addition to finding possible cases of asbestos-related disease in the hundreds and hundreds of people his firm screened, "we also identified thirty-two cases of lung cancer, one case of mesothelioma and twenty cases of nonasbestos-related cancer."

Perhaps they offered to help them sue someone too—anyone that's not already been bankrupted.

Certainly many workers have terrible diseases after being exposed to asbestos. Some were likely even the victims of uncaring employers who didn't pay attention to the dangers or didn't provide proper safety equipment. Those men and women are the true victims, the ones who should be asking for compensation. But with a quarter-million people—the 80 percent having no symptoms of anything—in line too, bankrupting their former employers and draining off insurance coverage with frivolous claims, what's the chance that the *real* victims will get their due?

You know that answer. Meanwhile, those without any sign of disease are stealing air from those who do.

Sources:

* "Asbestos Lawsuits Anger Critics," *St. Louis Post-Dispatch*, 9 February 2003
* "Asbestos Has Been Used Since Ancient Times," Asbestos Network.com (an "educational" Web site sponsored by the Brayton-Purcell law firm, which works on asbestos cases), undated.

Afterword:

Congress moved to limit asbestos legal cases, but it's not only a matter of "too little, too late" since so many companies were forced out of business, it's also a great ex-

Asbestos Litigation Crisis

In 2001 alone, seventy thousand new asbestos lawsuits were filed; more than eight thousand companies have been sued. On average, 61 percent of every award in asbestos cases goes to legal fees, leaving only 39 cents on the dollar for the plaintiffs.

Owens Corning alone had 460,000 asbestos claims filed against them, totaling $5 billion. They filed for bankruptcy in October 2000. Federal-Mogul went bankrupt in October 2000 after 365,000 claims, totaling $2.1 billion. Dozens of other companies were also bankrupted. It's estimated that the total of actual settlements paid out related to asbestos will top $200 billion—and $122 billion of that will go to the lawyers. (Source: *The Political Junkie*)

ample of a Band-Aid. Prohibit the whack-a-mole lawyers from trolling for asbestos "victims"? No problem: They'll pop up on other issues, such as suing fast-food restaurants for "forcing" obese people to eat junk food. The solution for outrageous abuse isn't to make that particular flavor of case illegal; the solution must be systemic.

Meanwhile, a team at Johns Hopkins University reviewed the actual X-rays used in court to win money in asbestos cases. Experienced radiologists who had no stake in the outcome found that only 4.5 percent of the 492 chest X-rays found "something wrong" with the patient. "Medical experts" hired by attorneys who reviewed the same X-rays had found 96 percent of the X-rays showed signs of illness. When it published the study, the medical journal *Academic Radiology* editorialized that it was time to "repair the breach" in the integrity of the profession, pointing out that the code of ethics of the American College of Radiology calls for members to exercise "extreme caution to ensure that the testimony provided is nonpartisan, scientifically correct and clinically accurate."

So how is it that radiologists hired by lawyers found twenty to twenty-five times the level of illness that a panel of disinterested reviewers did? Follow the money: Medical expert witnesses earn $600 to $800 per hour to testify at trials, and there's no trial if an "expert" doesn't swear he found signs of illness.

"If these people gave testimony that was incorrect, they should be prosecuted," said Dr. Michael Manco-Johnson, former head of radiology at the University of Colorado Health Sciences Center. "There are unscrupulous people in every field, but if they hook up with unscrupulous lawyers, this could very well happen." He added that "there are physicians who become professional testifiers, who get their entire salaries from it. They're usually very inadequate physicians, not very good at what they do, who can't make it practicing radiology." Those who lie in court, he says, are somewhere from "unethical to immoral."

Those choking to death from real lung diseases, but can't collect from bankrupt companies, would tend to agree.

Source:

* "Asbestos X-rays Rechecked; Study Casts Doubt on Medical Experts' Courtroom Testimony," *Rocky Mountain News,* 5 August 2004

1	*	) Location: Mississippi
2	Little Old Lady	) Year: 2002
3	v.	) Award Status: Runner-up
4	Her Doctor	) for the 2002 Stella Award
5		)

UNWANTED SIDE EFFECTS

When someone is truly harmed, sometimes a lawsuit is necessary to ensure that there is compensation for the harm done. But when greedy people jump on the bandwagon just for the money, they can cause true harm of their own.

The drug Propulsid (cisapride) was approved by the U.S. Food and Drug Administration in 1993 for treatment of a certain digestive disorder. But by the end of 1999, the drug was implicated in 341 cases of heart rhythm abnormalities, which have allegedly led to eighty deaths. Its manufacturer pulled Propulsid off the market—and lawsuits quickly followed.

Hazel Norton of Rolling Fork, Mississippi, read about the problems with Propulsid and stopped taking it. She decided to sue because, she said, "I might get a couple of thousand dollars." She apparently suffered no heart rhythm abnormalities from the drug. "Actually, I didn't get hurt by Propulsid," Norton admitted.

Norton's doctor, Kirk Kooyer, came to the Mississippi Delta to help poor people and, he says, to answer a Christian calling. His wife is also a doctor—a pediatrician and internist. Dr. Kooyer has "made an incredible difference in the health of women and children" of the region, said Dr. Chris Glick of the Mississippi-based National Perinatal Association. "He could have had a very well-to-do practice in Michigan but instead he chose to work in the poorest counties in Mississippi as a gift from his heart."

Dr. Kooyer and his wife are among the few doctors on staff at the Sharkey-Issaquena Community Hospital, where virtually all the patients are below the poverty level. Well, they *were* on staff: The doctor couple left Mississippi for North Dakota because, they said, they're tired of being sued. Dr. Kooyer's wife, Maria Weller, was the only pediatrician in a two-county area. Both have been sued before, and they claim the suits are without merit.

Only two doctors were left practicing at the hospital. "What's going to be hard is to find someone to replace [Dr. Kooyer] because whoever comes will face the same thing," said hospital administrator Winfred Wilkinson. "It's the patients who'll suffer." The Mississippi State Medical Association says about a hundred doctors left the state in 2002 alone.

Lawsuits are such a problem in Mississippi that a special session of the legislature was called to address the issue and try to stem the flow of doctors out of the state— they admit they are fleeing lawsuits and high malpractice insurance premiums. What do local lawyers say about it? Malpractice insurance premiums are rising "because of the economy and September 11," claimed trial lawyer Dennis Sweet of Jackson, presumably with a straight face. "It doesn't have anything to do with lawsuits."

Dr. Kooyer no doubt disagrees. His leaving made Hazel Norton "kind of upset," she said. "I do not want him leaving because of all the suits. If we run off all the doctors, what are the people gonna do?" Too late, lady. Even though she instructed her attorney to drop Dr. Kooyer from her lawsuit, he had already decided to move. Her lawyer had named him in the suit so the case would be tried in Mississippi, where juries are known to be generous about transferring money from "rich" insurance companies to poor people. Of course, the insurance companies then raise doctors' premiums to pay for the largesse, which puts more pressure on the doctors to leave.

Such lawsuits "are just the symptoms of a state in which key people have lost their ethical integrity," Dr. Kooyer said. When an overweight patient asked him for the diet drug fen-phen, he refused to give it to her, telling her in his opinion the drug combination was deadly. She went to another doctor for the drugs—and later got a $125,000 settlement from the fen-phen class-action lawsuit. The patient showed him the settlement check, he said. "I told you about the damage, and you decided to get the drugs anyway," he told her. "It doesn't seem fair for you to be accepting that check."

"Where has the shame gone?" Dr. Kooyer wonders. He's too polite to say the obvious: The shame has been sold by people like Hazel Norton for "a few thousand dollars." She admited she was not harmed by Propulsid, but she sued anyway to wrestle a piece of the pie from the people who were harmed. As a result of her greed, the poverty-stricken people around her will suffer from a lack of medical care. Maybe now Norton knows what a side effect is.

Sources:

* "Heartburn Drug Withdrawn; Propulsid Linked to Heart Rhythm Abnormalities," WebMD, 23 March 2000

* "Tort Reform: Just What the Doctor Ordered?" *Jackson Clarion-Ledger,* 29 July 2002

Afterword:

In September 2004 the popular arthritis drug Vioxx was pulled from the market, and instantly law firms rushed out ads looking for "victims" seeking to make a claim against its manufacturer, Merck. If you wonder why prescription drugs are so expensive, there's part of the answer for you. The more such cases we see, the less likely drug companies will try to tackle the diseases that ail us. That, ultimately, would be the tragedy of greedy opportunists trying to milk the system because for some reason they feel entitled to "a few thousand dollars" even though they suffered no injury. People like Hazel Norton don't just put their neighbors at risk, they put us all at risk.

School Daze
What Are Our Kids Really Learning?

Kids learn by example, and the examples adults set in court are rubbing off on them. What concerns kids the most these days? School. Not actually because it's the place where they learn, but because . . . it's so *unfair*! All these *rules*! And all that homework. What better revenge against teachers or the principal than to sue them?

```
1              *              )   Location: Michigan
                              )
2     System Manipulator      )   Year: 2003
                              )
3              v.             )   Award Status:
                              )   Dishonorable Mention
4        The System           )
                              )
5   ------------------------------)
```

LAWYER IN TRAINING

As part of his high school coursework, Brian Delekta, 18, worked in his mother's Memphis, Michigan, law office as a paralegal. The "work experience" class was even graded. His mother, Attorney Diane Delekta, said the school provided a "checklist" of things it required, and Brian accomplished those requirements.

He performed the same tasks he would do if he were a paralegal in a law office, she said. "He prepared documents, met with clients." As his supervisor, it was up to her to give him a grade in the class. She gave him an A+.

Since the highest grade the school district records is an A, that's what it put on his report card. When Brian protested, the Memphis School Board considered changing its grading system so it could record A+ grades. But the board voted against making such a change.

That, Brian figures, endangered his chances of being named class valedictorian, even though all the other students in his class followed the same rules he had to, so, with his mother's help, he filed a lawsuit against the St. Clair County Intermediate School District, all seven members of the school board, the school superintendent, and the high school's principal, demanding that the court order the school to increase his grade to an A+. In addition, it seeks a restraining order on class rankings until the school takes into account his higher grade. Oh, and $25,000 in cash, too, please.

"I heard ahead of time [that the threat of a lawsuit] was out there, but to worry about that would be wrong," said school board president Harold Burns. "I felt I did what was right for the citizens of Memphis" in voting against changing the grade system. The possibility of a restraining order against the school releasing grade rankings poses a real problem for others, he says: Students who need to know their class rank won't be able to apply for college scholarships until the court vacates the restraining order.

Clearly, Brian learned a lot while working at the law office, such as invoking hardball ploys like inconveniencing innocent third parties as a leveraging tactic. But St. Clair County Judge Daniel Kelly denied the motion for a restraining order, leaving the school free to issue class rankings. It named another student valedictorian, and Brian was named second in his class. The other aspects of the suit are apparently still pending.

Sources:

* "Student Files Lawsuit over School Grade: Memphis Pupil Believes He Deserves A+," *Port Huron Times Herald*, 6 February 2003
* "Memphis Releases Student Rankings," *Port Huron Times Herald*, 13 February 2003

Afterword:

The trial court threw the case out—and Delekta appealed. On October 12, 2004, the Michigan Court of Appeals affirmed the lower court's ruling, showing the state's
court system is fully capable of an A+ performance. Total
time from report card to final decision: more than two
years, by which time Brian was presumably a junior in
college.

```
1              *            )  Location: New Jersey
2    My Daddy's a Judge     )  Year: 2003
                            )
3           v.              )  Award Status:
4       Her School         )  Dishonorable Mention
5                          )
```

FIRST IN LINE

It may not be a big surprise that Moorestown, New Jersey, high school senior Blair L. Hornstine, 18, wants to be a lawyer. She's clearly a good student: Her grade point average is 4.6894, including twenty-three A+ grades— the highest at her school. She scored 1570 (out of 1600) on her SAT (previously known as the Scholastic Aptitude Test), and was accepted by a distinguished roster of top universities, including Harvard, Stanford, Princeton, Duke, and Cornell. She chose Harvard.

But Moorestown High School Superintendent Paul Kadri thought that that two other students should also be eligible to be named valedictorian, since Hornstine had an "unfair advantage" over the other students—Hornstine is disabled with a type of chronic fatigue syndrome. Because of that, she was exempt from some of the classes other students had to take, such as physical education, which counted less for grade-point calculations. She was also allowed to take some of her classes at home, which meant she was not "subject to the rigorous in-school grading standards employed by certain advanced placement teachers" as were the two other students, who also had near-perfect grades. And finally, she also got individualized attention from teachers, and extra time to take tests.

"After reviewing these issues, I was concerned about the fundamental fairness of the academic competition engaged in for the valedictorian and salutatorian awards," Kadri said. Thus, he concluded, "The level field of competition . . . had been compromised" to give Hornstine an edge. His suggestion: the school should name Hornstine and the other two students as "co-valedictorians."

Nothing doing, Hornstine said: She filed a discrimination suit in federal court asking for an order preventing the school from naming anyone but the student with the highest grade-point average as valedictorian.

"Not only does the conferral of co-valedictorian inaccurately suggest that Blair Hornstine was not at the top of her class," her suit argued, "but under the circumstances under which it is being conferred, it actually raises a derogatory implication that her superior performance is not what it seems."

Oh, and she'd also like $2.7 million, please—$200,000 in compensation for her "humiliation" and $2.5 million in punitive damages, payable to her from the taxpayers in the school district.

John Comegno, the school's attorney, argued that Hornstine would not suffer any loss by being named co-valedictorian. "She might be asked to share a stage, nothing more," he said. "We're just asking the court to level the playing field."

Hornstine's fellow students were behind the school, and called her "selfish." The *Philadelphia Inquirer* newspaper editorialized, "There's a saying that everything we need to know we learned in kindergarten. Blair Hornstine of

Moorestown must not have been paying attention the day her class learned about playing well with others." It called her "Little Miss Perfect" and "a petty crybaby," and wondered what lesson she was learning by suing—"that overcoming a disability and making it to the top is only worth celebrating if you're up there alone?" Tough words from a big newspaper to a young woman, but an accurate reflection of the community's feelings.

Ignoring public sentiment, U.S. District Court Judge Freda Wolfson agreed with Hornstine and ordered the school to name her the sole valedictorian. She said the school violated the girl's civil rights with its "strange and relentless" effort to discredit her. "If forced to share the award, the stigma would likely be unshakable," Wolfson ruled. "She would be seen as 'the disabled valedictorian,' not 'the valedictorian.' "

A trial to determine any monetary damages was set for later.

By demanding a huge economic windfall in her suit, Hornstine showed that her case wasn't so much about principle as profit. Instead of championing the rights of the disabled, she showed more that the disabled are on a par with everyone else in the greed department. Sadly, she won't be remembered for her very real scholastic accomplishments, but rather as a brat who got where she is by suing—she won't be remembered as "the disabled valedictorian" because she won't even be remembered as any sort of valedictorian; rather, she'll simply be known as "the girl that sued." She may have won in federal court, but in the eyes of the Court of Public Opinion she's a loser indeed—and so are thousands of other hardworking disabled students who just want to be recognized as regular human beings.

Sources:

* "Student Sues over Top Title," *Philadelphia Inquirer*, 2 May 2003
* "Disabled S. Jersey Senior Is Ruled Sole Valedictorian," *Philadelphia Inquirer*, 9 May 2003
* "Student's Lawsuit Shows Lack of Class," *Philadelphia Inquirer* (editorial), 3 May 2003

Afterword:

"The stigma would be unshakable," the judge ruled in this case. How prophetic those words were. The Hornstine case is an excellent case study in how things can go wrong for a plaintiff, even when she wins.

First, it was revealed that during her high school career, Hornstine wrote six articles for the Cherry Hill (New Jersey) *Courier-Post* newspaper, and all but one, the newspaper said after reviewing them, contained plagiarized material.

Hornstine's articles "had information from sources that was not properly attributed," the paper said in an editor's note to its readers. "The articles and essays had passages and themes from online sources that were not identified." It said that Hornstine copied passages from a U.S. Supreme Court opinion, writings from Supreme Court Justice William Brennan, portions of two proclamations by President Bill Clinton, and sections from other sources.

The stories ran under Hornstine's byline, implying she had written the words herself. "The *Courier-Post*'s Principles of Ethical Conduct for the Newsroom calls for proper attribution of specific language taken from another source and used in the newspaper," the editor told readers. In her defense, Hornstine argued that "all knowledge is constructed upon scholarship bequeathed to us by past generations," but acknowledged the "importance" of citing the work of others. She said in school she learned to do that using endnotes or footnotes and thought "news articles didn't require as strict citation scrutiny as most school assignments because there was no place for footnotes or endnotes."

Naturally, one of Hornstine's lawyers jumped into the act to point out that she "was not provided with a copy of the *Courier-Post*'s Principles of Ethical Conduct," as if a senior honors student wouldn't already know it was wrong to plagiarize. Moorestown School Superintendent Paul Kadri said he couldn't comment on Hornstine's plagiarism, or whether the school would review her academic work to check for plagiarism, because her $2.7 million civil suit was still pending. However, he did say all students "should know to give proper attribution in their work"—just as Hornstine admits. In her lawsuits, Hornstine insisted that the school follow its rules to the letter so that she would be named the school's sole valedictorian. But apparently that's not so important when the rules apply to her.

Sadly, the notoriety was too much for Hornstine: Despite her victory awarding her sole valedictorian status, she decided not to attend her graduation after all. Her lawyer, Edwin Jacobs, told the school that this was because "the hostile environment at the school has traumatized Blair both physically and emotionally, to the point that she cannot and will not attend the graduation ceremonies." He further asked the school to "please arrange to have the valedictorian award made to her in absentia," apparently forgetting that the primary duty of a valedictorian is to give a speech to the graduating class.

The *Philadelphia Daily News* noted, "The court victory guaranteed that Hornstine, 17, would be the one and only valedictorian at Moorestown. But it has also given rise to an ugly backlash in the court of public opinion that has shamed and cracked the veneer of civility in the quaint, affluent town." Further proof indeed that it's a very bad idea to show contempt for the Court of Public Opinion.

More to the point, is such sloppy attribution the mark of a scholar? Harvard didn't think so: It rescinded her acceptance to the university. Harvard officials refused to discuss "specific applicants," but a spokesman noted the school has a right to rescind admission to students who exhibit "behavior that brings into question your honesty, maturity, or moral character." Apparently, plagiarism by a supposedly top student isn't evidence of the honesty, maturity, and moral character Harvard seeks. Perhaps also a history of suing one's school in a fit of self-righteous indignation was another point against her.

By August of her graduation year Hornstine had settled her suit, wrangling $60,000 from her school. Her lawyers' fees: $45,000. Her net take-away for ruining her reputation, becoming an international laughingstock, making enemies of all of her classmates, and losing her spot at Harvard: $15,000. She was so despised for her suit she didn't attend her own graduation, and thus didn't fulfill her primary responsibility as valedictorian.

So congratulations to Blair: After a several-month fight, she "won." Whoopie. Is it really prognostication to say that her next trip to court may be to fight the IRS?

Sources:

* "Stories, Essays Lacked Attribution," *Cherry Hill Courier-Post*, 3 June 2003
* "A Valedictorian Is Confronted by a Fresh Difficulty," *Philadelphia Inquirer*, 5 June 2003
* "Court-Ordered Valedictorian Will Skip Graduation," *Philadelphia Daily News*, 11 June 2003
* "Harvard Bids Bye-bye to Blair," *Philadelphia Daily News*, 12 July 2003
* "Hornstine Settles Suit Against Moorestown School District," *Philadelphia Inquirer*, 19 August 2003

A Taxing Problem

Blair Hornstine's $15,000 award is before taxes. Doug Thorburn, an enrolled agent (tax specialist) in California, said she indeed has to pay taxes on the winnings, "but not on the $15,000; she has to declare the entire $60K judgment as income! And even worse, attorney's fees for such lawsuits are not deductible for purposes of calculating the Alternative Minimum Tax (AMT) in some Circuit Court of Appeal districts, including hers. In almost every situation and tax bracket, Hornstine would fail to receive the benefit of most of a disallowed-for-AMT deduction as large as this. In fact, for many, the deduction would save nothing. Assuming Hornstine has no other income or deductions (which, as a student, is reasonably likely), the AMT would be $5,135 vs. a regular tax of $1,443. Therefore, her overall net compensation would be $9,685—$15,000 minus $5,135. But if she's in the maximum combined federal/New Jersey state income tax brackets and the legal fees don't help as a deduction, she'll pay $24,840 in income tax, for a net *loss* of $9,480. The good news from her point of view is that many believe the IRS position on the deductibility of attorney's fees incurred for the production of such income to be wrong-headed. The issue is long overdue for a Supreme Court review. However, occasionally an unjust interpretation of tax law provides a measure of justice in areas we wouldn't expect, including that of most lawsuits deserving of a Stella Award in which the plaintiff wins." (*Source: e-mail interview with Doug Thorburn, EA*)

```
1              *              )   Location: California
2   Wanna-be Baseball Star   )   Year: 2003
                              )
3              v.             )   Award Status: Runner-up
4         His School          )   for the 2003 Stella Award
                              )
5   ------------------------- )
```

WHIFF?

When he was just 17, Cole Bartiromo made a killing in the stock market—using, the U.S. Securities and Exchange Commission says, fraudulent schemes over the Internet.

The SEC filed charges in two sets of cases. In one, the SEC said, Bartiromo artificially inflated stock prices in a pump-and-dump scheme. In the second, he ran an investment company that offered "guaranteed" profits of up to 2,500 percent over a few days or weeks, but (obviously) didn't deliver them. Without admitting guilt, Bartiromo turned over about $1.2 million in profits. SEC fines are apparently still pending against him.

That wasn't the only penalty, however: Bartiromo, a high school student, played left field on his school's varsity baseball team, and the school kicked him off the team.

Thanks to the SEC's case, Bartiromo gained firsthand experience as to how the court system works. "I've seen plenty," he said, such as "motions, court filings, everything." Wouldn't a smart kid like that want to put such hard-earned knowledge to work? You bet.

Acting as his own attorney, Bartiromo sued Trabuco

Hills High School in Mission Viejo, California, for not letting him play baseball. According to his lawsuit, filed in U.S. District Court in Santa Ana, his "civil rights" were violated by not being allowed to play, since college recruiters and professional team scouts couldn't see how good he was out there in left field. That meant the school destroyed his "potential baseball career" and, consequently, his multimillion-dollar professional ballplayer salary. He demands $50 million in compensation for those "lost earnings."

Bartiromo, who was 18 when he filed his suit, claimed that the banishment from the team was based on "personal vendettas" against him by the school's administrators because of their "jealousy/anger/spite of Bartiromo's local fame." He lost an appeal at the time, but his lawsuit alleges he was denied "due process" because all the members of the athletic review board were "against him" and no baseball coaches were included. He had accepted that decision at the time, but now says that acceptance was "coerced."

The suit, which Bartiromo wrote himself, includes a litany of other charges, including being called to the school's office to answer charges of "bogus infractions" and having some personal details about him removed from the school yearbook. "Instead of savoring every final moment of that final year to remember, Bartiromo has been left with thoughts of horror and the discrimination he endured," he complains in his suit.

Bartiromo claimed the SEC is seeking a "nine-figure" ($100 million or more) penalty against him in his still-pending fraud cases. "I wish we could get this over with so I can move on," he said. "I can't do anything until this is settled. I'm just sitting on pins and needles here."

With the SEC looking over his shoulder, Bartiromo is

staying away from a stock market career. And with his potential baseball career shot, what does he plan to do for a
living? (No, he doesn't plan to become an attorney.) That's
right: He hopes to become a rap artist.

"I have a story to tell like no other," he said, without any
hint of a rhyme. "Every other musician's story is a rags-
to-riches story. They whine about poverty then make it
big. I had it all, I was at the top and I'm now hitting rock
bottom. The only way to express that is through rap and
hip-hop."

Well, that and through frivolous eight-figure lawsuits,
as well.

Sources:

* "Teen in Internet Fraud Cases Sues School for $50 Million,"
  Los Angeles Times, 17 May 2003
* "SEC Files More Charges Against California Teen," Associ-
  ated Press, 29 April 2002
* "Litigation Release No. 17296," U.S. Securities and Ex-
  change Commission, 7 January 2002

Afterword:

Bartiromo can't seem to leave fraud behind. In 2004 he
pleaded guilty to federal conspiracy and bank fraud
charges for selling items on eBay that he never delivered,
and for trying to get a bank employee to "loan" him
$400,000 from another customer's account, which would
be used to "gamble on the Internet." He then promised to
return the money "before the account holder was aware
the money was missing." The bank employee instead called
police. Bartiromo was sentenced to thirty-three months in

prison; the maximum sentence he faced was thirty-five years.

Sources:

* "Three Charged in Calif. Bank Scheme," Associated Press, 29 January 2004
* "SoCal Teen Pleads Guilty to Conspiracy and Bank Fraud Charges," Associated Press, 2 March 2004

```
1               *            )   Location: North Carolina
2            Slacker         )   Year: 2003
                             )
3              v.            )   Award Status:
                             )   Dishonorable Mention
4       College Entrance     )
                             )
5        Requirements        )
                             )
```

CLASSLESS OF 2008

Mark Edmonson, 18, was doing pretty well at Northwest Guilford High School in Greensboro, North Carolina. Early in his senior year, he had a 3.8 grade-point average, scored a perfect 1600 on his SAT, was a National Merit finalist, and, outside school, had incorporated his own Internet company. Combined, that made him a shoo-in at the college of his choice, the University of North Carolina in Chapel Hill.

UNC sent him a letter of acceptance in April 2003. However, the letter warned, "your enrollment will depend upon your successful completion of your current academic year." Further, it said, "We expect you to continue to achieve at the same level that enabled us to provide this offer of admission; we also expect you to graduate on time."

Edmonson graduated on time, but that's about all—in his final semester he earned only C and D grades, and failed one class entirely, dropping his overall GPA to 3.5. Not surprisingly, UNC was unhappy, but rather than rescinding Edmonson's admission it "temporarily suspended" it and asked him to come in for an interview to discuss the matter. Apparently unsatisfied with the answers after the interview, UNC did rescind Edmonson's acceptance, though it suggested he might consider "transferring to Carolina after you have established a record of success at another college or university."

But Edmonson only wanted to go to UNC. Once he got its April acceptance he not only slacked off in high school, he didn't bother to apply anywhere else. "If they say he can't come, I don't know what we'll do," said his mother, Barbara. "We're kind of stuck."

Edmonson wasn't satisfied with "stuck": He called Marshall Hurley, an attorney. In a lawsuit filed in Orange County Superior Court in Hillsborough, Hurley argues the university's admission letter was a binding contract both parties agreed to. Thus UNC's rescinding the offer is an unjustified "breach of contract." It asks the court to order UNC to allow him to start classes immediately.

The suit claims the university didn't give Edmonson a chance to explain what happened in his in-person interview, but admissions director Herb Davis differs. "He looked at his transcript and responded to my question of what happened to him with philosophical quotes but nothing directly related to my questions," Davis wrote in a formal affidavit in response to the suit.

Attorney Hurley sees it differently: "I frankly think that his 1600 [SAT] score was being held against him, that even with his lofty score, they can teach him a lesson," he said. "I just think there's some arrogance going on here, some bureaucratic arrogance."

Beyond the rather laughable claim that an institution of higher learning would hold academic achievement against a student, would Hurley also consider it "arrogance" to accept the terms of a "contract" and then fail to live up to them? The acceptance letter made it clear what his client had to do to be admitted to UNC—the clearly laid out "terms" of the so-called "contract" letter—but he didn't do it. If there's a "breach of contract" here, Edmonson is the one who breached it. By failing to have any sort of backup plan to implement as he saw his grades slipping, and by putting all his energy into a lawsuit rather than applying to other schools, Edmonson only proved one thing: He's not the sort of scholar a university like UNC prefers to walk through its halls.

Apparently Edmonson's case wasn't strong enough for an injunction—the judge refused to grant a court order forcing the school to admit him. However, the judge didn't throw out the suit, so it will be heard in due time. Meanwhile, Edmonson won't be going to school, his mother says. "The general feeling is just so negative that I'm not sure what he can do or where he can go," she said. "I can't imagine any admissions person in the area, at N.C. State or Duke or anywhere, even looking at him." He'll never know unless he tries, but it looks like Edmonson gave up long ago. And isn't that the entire problem?

Sources:

* "UNC Admission Rescission Sparks Suit," *Durham Herald-Sun,* 19 August 2003
* "Rejected Student Ponders Future," *Durham Herald-Sun,* 22 August 2003

```
1              *            )  Location: Iowa
                            )
2        Cheerleader        )  Year: 2003
                            )
3            v.             )  Award Status:
                            )  Dishonorable Mention
4        Landing Pad        )
                            )
5  -------------------------
```

THE INEVITABLE SPREAD
OF AMERICAN LEGAL
IDEAS

Jenny Lawson of Eccleshall, England, attended Roosevelt High School in Des Moines, Iowa, as an exchange student. As a member of the school cheerleading squad, she was performing a jump and ran into another cheerleader. She fell and broke her leg.

On the face of it, it sounds like it was her fault. Shall we chalk it up to a simple accident? No, she says: The school is negligent for failing to require cheerleaders to do their stunts on "absorbent mats" and "encouraging more than one cheerleader to jump at once." Therefore she has sued the Des Moines School District seeking unspecified monetary damages.

The district's attorney said he doesn't know of any school that has a requirement for "absorbent mats." Further, he said, cheerleading is a sport that carries "an inherent risk of injury." Even in England Lawson should have learned to "look before she leaps"—or isn't there such a thing as accidents in England anymore?

Source:

* "Foreign Exchange Student Files Suit," *Des Moines Register,* 2 January 2003

Offshoring

"Predatory Litigation: 70 percent of the world's lawyers reside in the U.S. and 94 percent of the world's lawsuits are filed in the States. Litigation on commission is illegal everywhere in the world except the U.S. A new lawsuit is filed every thirty seconds in America already, and there are now more law students in school than [lawyers] in actual practice."

—Part of what U.S. companies can avoid by moving out of the country, as promoted by "The Offshore Advantage" Web site.

That's Just Stupid
Or, Don't Tell <u>Me</u> I Don't Get My Day in Court!

Some suits are just too stupid to believe. How can any judge entertain such a suit? How did the lawyer keep a straight face when he accepted the case? Yet they weren't necessarily thrown out of court immediately. You have to wonder: Why not?

```
1                 *              )  Location: Iowa
                                 )
2         Jilted Lover          )  Year: 2003
                                 )
3              v.               )  Award Status:
                                 )  Dishonorable Mention
4        Former Lover          )
                                 )
5   --------------------------------
```

UNLUCKY IN LOVE

Joseph Bisignano, 66, of Des Moines, Iowa, spent two years—and, he said, more than $330,000—in an attempt to convince Mary Toon, 54, to become his fourth wife. He said she wanted a formal engagement party, so he bought her a designer wedding dress and a $75,000 engagement ring.

Alas, Toon threw him over . . . shortly after he bought her a $4,000 fur coat. In response, Bisignano has sued Toon, alleging fraud, breach of contract, and "unjust enrichment." The suit demands the return of $129,000 worth of gifts, plus $201,259 cash for loans and purchases Bisignano made for her.

Toon's lawyer said the "mere allegations" won't stand up in court, and that there was no "relationship as he described it." That's one way to avoid a fourth painful divorce: Get it over with early!

Source:

* "West Des Moines Man Sues to Regain Money He Spent on Woman," *Des Moines Register,* 6 January 2003

```
1                  *            )  Location: Iowa
                               )
2   Antisocial Celebrants      )  Year: 2003
                               )
3              v.              )  Award Status:
                               )  Dishonorable Mention
4      Their Getaway Car       )
                               )
5   ------------------------------)
```

OK, LADY, WHERE'S THE FIRE?

On the Fourth of July, 2002, Tanya Whitaker rented a Chevy Blazer from Enterprise Rent-A-Car in Des Moines, Iowa. With her fiancé Tyson Wells, his brother and sister Teondra and Doug Wells, and friends O'Keitha Nelson and Shunntae Averette, Whitaker drove to a neighborhood known for its Independence Day "fireworks wars"—where people shoot fireworks at each other.

As Whitaker drove, Tyson and Doug shot bottle rockets out the vehicle's windows at people. At one point Tyson tried to shoot a rocket out the window, but instead it exploded inside the car and set off the cache of fireworks in the passenger compartment, including Roman candles.

Doug suffered burns over 23 percent of his body; Teondra 60 percent. Averette, just 15 years old, died.

Who should be to blame for the tragedy? While Averette's estate accepted a settlement from Whitaker's auto insurance carrier, Teondra and Doug decided to sue Whitaker; they also sued Enterprise Rent-A-Car, under the theory that Iowa law holds a vehicle's owner liable for damages caused by the driver.

Not surprisingly, Enterprise argued that the law is meant to assign blame for injuries caused by the vehicle itself, not the actions of its driver or passengers. An Iowa jury agreed, assigning 20 percent of the blame for the accident to Whitaker and 80 percent to Tyson, who caused the accident in the first place. In a fit of common sense, they held Enterprise blameless for actions it had absolutely no ability to control.

Source:

* "Auto Renter Not Liable for Fireworks," *National Law Journal,* 8 November 2002

Small Business

Tort reform is often thought of as a cure for what ails big business. Not so, according to a study of lawsuit impacts on *small* businesses (defined as having less than $10 million in annual revenue and at least one employee in addition to the owner). The toll on them is about $88 billion a year, or 68 percent of business tort liability costs. The average small business with $10 million in revenue spends $150,000 on tort liability costs.

The picture for very small businesses (defined as having less than $1 million in annual revenue and at least one employee in addition to the owner) is even worse. Their total tort liability price tag is $33 billion per year, or 26 percent of business tort liability costs. The average small business with $1 million in revenue spends $17,000 on tort liability costs. Of their $33 billion "share," 44 percent is paid out of pocket, not from insurance, either because they have none or because their insurance coverage is not adequate to cover judgments. (*Source: NERA Economic Consulting*)

```
1              *              )  Location: West Virginia
2       Crime Victims         )  Year: 2003
                              )
3            v.               )  Award Status:
                              )  Dishonorable Mention
4       Rehab Efforts         )
5  ---------------------------)
```

JAILHOUSE BLUES

Jason Henthorne is in prison in West Virginia for murdering Michael Hart. Cable TV music channel VH1 produced a show called *Music Behind Bars* about musical prison inmates. Among other criminals, it featured Henthorne and his music in one segment.

That upset his murder victim's mother, Linda Garrett, and his sister, Misty Hart. They demanded that VH1 scrap the show, but the cable channel aired it anyway. Garrett and Misty Hart thus sued Viacom, the corporate owner of VH1, claiming "emotional distress" from the show. They demand unspecified damages, plus unspecified punitive damages, plus a court order prohibiting VH1 from ever running the show again.

"Our case is alleging that despite repeated requests not to air the show, VH1 went ahead and it did it anyway," said attorney Liz Thompson, who represents the family. "A criminal who has harassed this family is being celebrated as someone of merit and it's causing the family to feel more harassed," agreed cocounsel Cy Weiner, adding that "VH1 is assisting in harassing the family. This is a victim's rights case, primarily. And it's an example of corporate irresponsibility."

Were the producers trying to glorify criminals? Hardly. The *Music Behind Bars* series was produced by Arnold Shapiro, who made the Oscar-winning 1978 prison documentary *Scared Straight*, which was designed to, well, scare kids into going "straight" and not committing crimes.

"I'm not fond of criminals," Shipiro said. "It was never our intention to make heroes of these criminals, just to show that a music program in a prison has many beneficial arenas to it. Music programs in whatever form they take actually benefit the prison itself. They focus the men and women on something positive. It contributes to rehabilitation of the criminal."

Maybe, and maybe not. There's only one way for the public to decide the issue, though: The issues and facts need public airing. So how does it serve the public interest to attempt to censor an exploration of what's going on in publicly funded prisons so that citizens can have an informed opinion on the subject? Indeed, that's what the First Amendment is all about: the right to look into a public institution and tell people about it. The plaintiffs weren't hurt by Viacom, they were hurt by a murderer. Their anger is misplaced, and their action threatens the ideal of an informed society.

Source:

* "Murder Victim's Family Sues VH1," Fox News, 6 March 2003

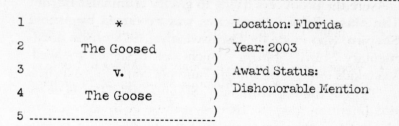

1   *   )   Location: Florida

2   The Goosed   )   Year: 2003

3   v.   )   Award Status:

4   The Goose   )   Dishonorable Mention

5   )

DUCK‼

In Florida, it's not unusual for alligators to pop out of the water—they've even been known to attack humans.

But that's not what bothered Darlene Griffin. The 30-year-old woman was in Okeeheelee Park in West Palm Beach when she was "attacked" by a different kind of water creature: a goose. Griffin says she jumped between her young son and the bird to protect the boy, then fell down and broke her tailbone when the fowl tried to bite her.

She sued Palm Beach County for allowing the wild animal to roam free in a public park. The suit asks for at least $15,000 to cover her medical bills, as well as her "mental and physical anguish." Griffin's attorney Joe Fields said that county officials later removed several geese from the park, including the one that attacked his client—which shows the geese are dangerous, he said. So according to him, the county was wrong to let a wild animal exist in the park, yet removing it proves it's at fault. In America's civil courts you're damned if you don't, and *really* damned if you do.

Sources:

* "Woman Suing County after Goose Run-in," *Palm Beach Post,* 24 January 2003
* "Woman Sues Palm Beach County over Attack by Goose at Okeeheelee Park," *South Florida Sun-Sentinel,* 24 January 2003

1	*	)	Location: Pennsylvania
2	Victims	)	Year: 2003
3	v.	)	Award Status:
4	Practical Joker	)	Rescinded Mention
5		)	

I'LL BE YOUR (SUBPOENA) SERVER TODAY

In April 2002, a man had breakfast at an International House of Pancakes restaurant in Philadelphia. After eating, he went to the manager and said he could not pay, and would they take an IOU instead? The man wouldn't identify himself and said he had no money or credit cards, but offered to wash dishes to pay off his debt.

Nervous since the restaurant had recently been robbed, the manager called 911. Hearing the words "refusing to pay" and "recent robbery," the police department dispatched Officer Thomas K. O'Neill with lights and siren through morning rush-hour traffic to confront the man. O'Neill had also responded to the earlier robbery.

"When the male continually refused to pay for the breakfast, the officer informed him that he would be placed under arrest," said Philly police spokesman Inspector William Colarulo. Once the subject of arrest was brought up, the man "jumped up and screamed that it was a . . . practical joke, that he worked for" a local radio station.

The man turned out to be Diego Ramos, 31, an on-air personality at WIOQ-FM morning radio in Philadelphia.

Not only that, but the "practical joke" was being broadcast live on the air via a hidden microphone plugged into Ramos's cell phone.

"This was a prank that we don't consider funny," spokesman Colarulo said. "The manager of the IHOP was acting in good faith by calling 911." Colarulo noted the officer "handled everything by the book," while Ramos "deliberately tried to bait [the] officer into some type of altercation while this was being broadcast." Ramos was released by the officer after radio station personnel—who were listening in—called the restaurant and gave them a credit card number to pay the bill.

Colarulo said the case was "being investigated as a criminal incident" and noted that if Ramos were to be arrested, "we do not take IOUs for bail." But after reviewing the case, the district attorney declined to file any charges. In an interview later, Ramos apologized "if we inconvenienced anyone."

Well over a year later, the silly stunt was long forgotten, right?

Wrong.

Stephen R. Lee, the owner of the restaurant, filed suit in Montgomery County Court seeking unspecified damages from Ramos, the radio station, and the station's corporate owner, Clear Channel Communications.

At the same time, Philadelphia Police Officer Thomas K. O'Neill separately filed suit in Philadelphia Common Pleas Court against the station and Clear Channel, asking for a minimum of $50,000 against claims he was defamed "in that his unwilling participation in the joke publicly made him look foolish and made him out to be a buffoon." Further, his suit says, "he was publicly and personally embarrassed and humiliated and that his authority as a Philadelphia police officer was degraded."

Yes, it was a stupid radio stunt, and some DJ-inspired stunts are getting way out of hand—and the radio stations don't care, since "any" publicity tends to be "good" publicity as far as they're concerned. But if the restaurant was harmed, it was because the manager overreacted to a man who offered an unconventional approach to paying his debt—the diner did not, after all, attempt to walk out without paying.

And how was the officer harmed? Even the department said in public that he "handled everything by the book." So was he really "personally embarrassed and humiliated" to have it revealed that he does his job correctly? If he had handled the situation improperly, the radio station would have been doing a public service to expose him, but he passed their test with flying colors. One would think there would be significantly more "embarrassment" by using a public forum—a courtroom—to cash in on a claim of victimization, thus holding up every cop in the city to the ever-more "humiliating" concept that a sixteen-year veteran officer cannot take a joke, and is still crying in his cruiser after more than a year.

Sources:

* "Radio Prankster's Stunt Was in Questionable Taste, Police Say," *Philadelphia Inquirer,* 6 April 2002
* "Radio Prank Does Not Go Over Easy," *Philadelphia Inquirer,* 15 June 2003

Afterword:

This case turned out to be interesting in that it was the first time I ever rescinded a Stella Award. After it was published online, several readers objected, noting that it's *illegal* for a radio station to secretly put people on the air like this. An arbitrator in the police officer's case agreed: The cop was awarded $1,000 in damages plus, because the broadcast was illegal, $3,000 in punitive damages, plus $20,000 for attorney's fees. Clear Channel, which owns the station, says it "completely disagrees with the ruling and will appeal." The suit by the restaurant is still pending. Total elapsed time for the officer's case: twenty-eight months.

Source:

* "Q102 Told After IHOP Prank: Check, Please," *Philadelphia Inquirer,* 8 August 2004

Awards Are Increasing

In addition to the increasing number of lawsuits filed in the U.S., the amounts awarded are also increasing, sometimes dramatically. Two examples:

Medical Malpractice

Year	Median Award
1996	$473,000
1999	$712,000
2002	$1,010,000

Product Liability

Year	Median Award
1996	$675,000
1999	$1,500,000
2002	$1,800,000

(*Source: Swiss Re, Jury Verdict Research*)

```
1                    *              )  Location: Oregon
                                    )
2       Doggedly Determined         )  Year: 2003
                                    )
3               v.                  )  Award Status: Runner-up
                                    )  for the 2003 Stella Award
4           Dog-Sitter              )
                                    )
5   ---------------------------------)
```

A DOG-EAT-DOG WORLD

Doug Baker, 45, of Portland, Oregon, said he met Fremont while driving four years ago. The German shepherd was in the road, cars swerving around him. He was limping. Baker said he believes God steered him to the dog, and he stopped to pick the animal up. "Our eyes met, and we connected," he says. "My life's never been the same."

Baker spent $4,000 in vet bills to get the dog well. "People thought I was crazy," he remembered, "but I'm telling you, God wanted me to save him."

Baker, who lived on a houseboat, would leave the dog with Lisa Klein, his girlfriend, during the night and bring him to his office during the day. "He was with one of us nearly twenty-four hours a day, and he really only trusted us," he said. "He was scared of people." Indeed the dog had a "reputation" for lunging and snapping at strangers.

When he had to go out, Baker would hire a dog-sitter. In September, Baker took Klein to dinner and paid the dog-sitter $30 to watch Fremont. When they got home, they found a message from the sitter: Fremont had run away. A truck driving by backfired and scared the skittish dog, and he got out of the yard—through an open gate, Baker alleged.

Baker went far beyond the usual procedure of looking for the dog and putting "lost and found" ads in the newspaper. He bought a display ad so he could include a photo. He offered a $1,000 reward. He circulated fliers and put up a Web site.

Then it gets drastic. He let his auto repair shop go out of business so he could devote himself full-time to the search. To pay the search expenses, he started taking early disbursements from his retirement fund. He says he had planned to ask Klein to marry him by tying an engagement ring to Fremont's collar so he could "deliver" it to her, but since the dog wasn't there to do that, he postponed the engagement.

Then it gets weird. Baker hired an animal tracker to follow the dog's scent. The tracker declared the dog had been abducted, so Baker hired four different "animal psychics" to divine where the dog was. Each session cost $55 to $100, and every one of them said they "communicated" with the animal. But when their leads came to a dead end, Baker hired a witch to cast spells to bring Fremont home.

Then it gets scary. "I went out and put my own urine in the area where Fremont was last seen," Baker says, reasoning "he might smell my scent and then stay put."

By day sixty, Baker had spent over $20,000 on finding Fremont. Shortly after that, the *Portland Oregonian* newspaper ran a long story on his search, just as Baker was ready to hire a fifth psychic. The story noted he cries over Fremont every day, and has a hard time going into his dining room because of memories of Fremont being in there.

But Baker got his happy ending: Two days after the

newspaper article ran, someone who saw the story phoned in a tip. Baker went to the neighborhood the tipster suggested and found Fremont in the street, about two miles from where he had disappeared. Baker's vet says the dog very likely roamed the area for the two months he was gone—he was apparently not "abducted" at all.

Well, that's not really the end—if it was, this wouldn't be the True Stella Awards. That's right: Baker sued.

Although upon finding Fremont he told the newspaper, "All I want to do now is rebuild my life," apparently he wanted someone else to pay for that rebuilding. Two days after getting the dog back, Baker and Klein hired Geordie Duckler, a Portland attorney who says he's the only Oregon attorney to specialize in the legal representation of pet owners. Duckler bragged that he has fifty open cases and has represented animals from birds to alligators.

Duckler filed suit against Lisa Dunbar, the pet-sitter, in Multnomah County Circuit Court demanding $160,000: $20,000 for the cost of Baker's search, $30,000 for the income he lost by letting his business collapse, $10,000 for "the temporary loss of the special value of Fremont based on his qualities, characteristics and pedigree," and $100,000 in "emotional damages."

"I lived a nightmare," Baker said. "Yesterday was the first day I didn't cry, and last night was the first night I didn't go out and scream."

At a news conference, Duckler said he hopes the lawsuit "helps redefine personal-property laws," saying pet-sitters should be held to "a higher standard of care" than people watching, say, someone's car.

Dunbar of course has hired an attorney to help defend her, and said her lawyer told her not to comment on the case. "All I can say is they are lying," she told the *Oregon-*

ian, "and they're taking advantage of the media." While the suit says she didn't do enough to help find Fremont, she said she "was out looking from the minute it happened. I even took time off from work to help look."

People indeed can form close, loving, even deep bonds with their pets. But who thinks it's reasonable to spend over $20,000 to find a lost dog, and let their business fail in the meantime? Obviously one person did think it was worth it—and that's his decision to make. Once he made that decision, he needs to live with its consequences. He knew his dog was skittish around strangers. The newspaper reported that the first thing he did when he found the dog was put a collar on him; didn't he take the most basic precaution of having tags on the dog all along so that if he did get lost, his owner could be found? And if it was "God's will" for him to find the dog in the first place, why wasn't it "God's will" for him to lose it later? Perhaps Baker "lived a nightmare," but now he has gone and created a far, far worse nightmare for the woman who tried to look after his cowering animal. Surely that's not part of God's plan.

Sources:

* "Looking for Fremont," *Portland Oregonian,* 30 November 2003
* "Love, Search for Dog Priceless in End," *Portland Oregonian,* 4 December 2003
* "Owner Sues Pet Sitter in Loss of Dog," *Portland Oregonian,* 6 December 2003

Afterword:

The suit was settled for an undisclosed amount thirteen months after the dog was lost.

My favorite reader letter on this case: "Let me get this straight: Mr. Baker spent $20,000 of his own money and let his business go under in order to find the dog that essentially *ran away from him*? He, an adult man, cried *daily* and avoided certain rooms in his house over a skittish dog? He hired multiple psychics and a witch? Did God steer him toward them as well? Not to downplay the strong emotional bond that can exist between an owner and pet, but quite frankly, Ms. Dunbar should settle out of court by offering to pay Mr. Baker's psychiatric bills. I think this would benefit him more in working through his 'emotional anguish' than $100K would. I mean, come on, this is a man who admitted to marking his territory with his own urine."

This is just a guess, but Ms. Dunbar would probably scoff at that idea, claiming that paying the $100K would be cheaper than paying Baker's psychiatric bills. . . .

```
1              *              )  Location: Georgia
                              )
2            Kids             )  Year: 2002
                              )
3             v.              )  Award Status: Runner-up
                              )  for the 2002 Stella Award
4            Dad              )
                              )
5    ---------------------------)
```

I SAID <u>NOW</u>, DADDY?

Singer James "Godfather of Soul" Brown was briefly committed to a psychiatric hospital by his daughter Deanna Brown Thomas in 1998 for addiction to painkillers. Brown has since held a "grudge" against her and his other daughter, Yamma Brown Lumar, they allege. They say that when he got out of the hospital, Brown "vowed to the media that his daughters will never get a dime from him" and "James Brown has kept his word."

Gosh: Cut off in his will for locking him in a nuthouse? Well, that calls for strong action, so they did what any kid would do when cut off from Daddy's bank account: They sued him for more than $1 million, claiming that they are owed royalties on twenty-five of his songs which, they claim, they helped him write. Even though, at the time, they were children. For instance, when Brown's 1976 hit "Get Up Offa That Thing" was a chart-topper, the girls were aged 3 and 6.

"This is a sad scenario," said their lawyer. Yep: It's enough to make Brown switch genres to the blues.

Source:

* "Singer James Brown Sued by Daughters," Associated Press, 18 September 2002

```
1              *          )  Location: Ohio
                          )
2      Lottery Winner     )  Year: 2004
                          )
3           v.            )  Award Status:
                          )  Dishonorable Mention
4     Ticket Salesman     )
                          )
5                         )
```

LIGHTNING STRIKES
TWICE

Over a period of four years, John Struna bought forty to fifty-five tickets per game from the Convenient Food Mart in Cleveland, Ohio, in his attempts to win the Buckeye Five lottery. By his own estimates, he spent $125,000 per year on the tickets.

He finally beat the odds: On October 25, 2001, after buying fifty-two tickets with the same number, Struna won. Each ticket was worth $100,000—except, the Ohio Lottery Commission pointed out when he tried to cash them in, the fifty-two tickets didn't add up to $5.2 million, since the rules for the game limited the payout to $1 million total. And since there were actually fifty-three winning tickets for that game, that $1 million would be split fifty-three ways, leaving Struna with "only" $981,000.

Whose fault is it that Struna didn't understand the rules? Harry Singh, the owner of the Convenient Food Mart, said he gave Struna a copy of the lottery's rules. Struna even kept them, carrying them in his pocket, says Singh's lawyer, Gary Seewald.

Mardele Cohen, spokeswoman for the Ohio Lottery,

said the rules for games are clearly posted on signs provided to ticket retailers and on their Web site. Retailers
are not required to give copies of the rules to ticket buyers, so Singh actually did more than what was required of
him by giving Struna a printed copy.

Cohen added that it's reasonably common for an individual player to buy ten tickets in an attempt to get all of
the $1 million limit, "but when we saw that someone
bought fifty-two tickets, it didn't make any sense to us."

Attorney Seewald noted that every single ticket even
has the $1 million cap printed on it. Between that, the
rules folder, the signs, and the lottery's Web site, he said,
the lottery "does a fairly good job of publicizing their rules
and I think people have an obligation not to be damn
idiots."

Struna begs to differ. He said the Lottery Commission
didn't do enough to let people know there was a cap and,
as an official retailer, Singh should have discouraged him
from buying more than ten tickets with any particular
number combination on them. With the help of attorney
Andrew Kabat, he sued Singh in Cuyahoga County Common Pleas Court demanding $100,000 in compensation
for each winning ticket that was made worthless by the
lottery's rule. He also filed suit against the Ohio Lottery,
claiming false advertising, in the Ohio Court of Claims.

The case against the Lottery Commission was thrown
out, but the Common Pleas jury ruled against Singh and
awarded Struna $1.3 million. Singh's attorney said the
huge judgment "could literally destroy him."

Struna is appealing the dismissal of his case against the
lottery. Singh said he will appeal, too.

When faced with people wanting to buy something, lottery ticket retailers shouldn't have to question the patron to ensure they understand all the rules. The tickets had the relevant rule printed right on them, but Singh went further and gave a copy of the rules to Struna—who apparently chose not to read them. Should Singh have held Struna down and forced him to listen to him read the rules aloud? Of course not. But that's the sort of requirement the jury would have us believe is reasonable by awarding a "damn idiot" more than a million bucks for refusing to understand what he had chosen to do, even when given all the information he needed to make an intelligent choice.

Sources:

* "Lottery Player Wins Again, This Time in Court," *Cleveland Plain Dealer*, 25 March 2004
* "Store Owner to Appeal Jury's Lottery Decision," Associated Press, 26 March 2004

Afterword:

A detail was left out of my analysis that dramatically changes the flavor of the case. Quite a few readers didn't catch it; one pointed out, "Do not forget that the Convenient Food Mart received a cut of each—can we call them 'worthless'?—extra ticket sold to Struna. Had he never won, he might never have realized that that poor small businessman Singh was defrauding him at worst, profiting from Struna's ignorance at the least." Even a law student argued, "I wholeheartedly agree with you that store owners shouldn't have an obligation to ensure that every single customer understands the rules of a lottery game, but this case seems to present a situation where a store owner should have the obligation to ensure that a customer purchasing forty to forty-five useless tickets per game understands the limitations imposed by the rules. This store owner was knowingly enriching himself at the expense of someone who clearly didn't understand the rules."

No! It makes strategic sense to buy more than ten tickets: It assures the winner gets a bigger portion of the jackpot in case there is more than one winner, which in fact there was. The extra forty-two tickets Struna bought brought him bigger winnings over buying just ten. How? The math is easy: Each winning ticket was worth $100,000, with a cap of $1 million. If Struna had bought ten, and his were the only winners, he'd get $10/10$ of that million—all of it. But there was someone else who had a winning ticket, so Struna, if he had only bought ten tickets, would "only" have gotten $10/11$ of the million, or $909,090. However, because he bought fifty-two tickets, he got $52/53$ of the million, or $981,132—$72,041 more! So Struna literally sued for getting *more* money than he would have had the lottery retailer refused to sell him additional tickets—and certainly if that had happened, Struna would have sued him for missing out on the $72,000 bonus! But then, go back to the details: Struna was spending about $125,000 *per year* on these tickets; doesn't that pretty much define a "professional"-level player? Why should anyone have to "warn" a professional about his actions?

But that's what the court promotes here. Litigating away reason and enacting laws to "protect" people against their lack of common sense is taking away many of the freedoms this country was founded on. "Big Brother" must take care of you, since you are not capable of taking care of yourself—even if you're wealthy enough to have $125,000 a year to blow on lottery tickets.

Struna's appeal of the dismissal of his case against the lottery failed. Singh's appeal against the $1.3 million judgment against him is apparently still pending.

SLAPPs and Other Corporate Abuse
Another Side of the Coin

Tort reform is essentially a "conservative" (or Republican) issue in the sense that lawsuits often target "deep pockets"—corporations. (Though my take on it is different: I decry the lack of common sense and the inability to predict in advance whether what one is doing is "wrong" or not.) The other side of the coin is SLAPP cases, or Strategic Lawsuits Against Public Participation. Corporations can "SLAPP" at people or interest groups who sue them, or complain about their products by filing frivolous motions and lawsuits. The idea is to tie them up in court or bankrupt them with attorneys' fees, effectively shutting them up. Worse, the mere threat of a SLAPP suit can discourage critics from saying anything bad about a real public issue, effectively squelching dissenting voices. That is the sort of legal abuse that comes to mind for "liberal" (or Democratic) causes.

SLAPP suits are such an abuse of the law that twenty-three states have made them illegal. Referring to such cases, Judge J. Nicholas Colabella of New York's Supreme Court has said, "Short of a gun to the head, a greater threat to First Amendment expression can scarcely be imagined."

Of course, SLAPPs aren't the only way corporations can try to take advantage of the common citizen, as you will see.

1	*)	Location: California
2	Product Reviewee)	Year: 2003
3	v.)	Award Status: Runner-up
4	Product Reviewer)	for the 2004 Stella Award
5	)	

A SHARP SLAPP
IN THE FACE

San Francisco–based Sharper Image was founded in 1977 and is a successful catalog merchant and mall retailer. Consumers Union was founded in 1936 and is a nonprofit product testing organization dedicated to getting objective product information out to consumers via its magazine, *Consumer Reports*.

To perform its product tests, CU buys example products in retail stores (rather than accepting carefully selected samples from manufacturers) and puts them through exhaustive tests to answer the questions: Do the products do what they're advertised to do? Do they do it well? And how well do they work compared to competing products?

For an early 2002 review of home air filters, CU bought sixteen air-filtering units from a number of sources, including an Ionic Breeze air purifier system from Sharper Image. The Ionic Breeze is the company's best-selling product; analysts say it may account for half of Sharper Image's sales, accounting for hundreds of millions of dollars of their income. Five different models sell in the range of $200 to $500.

To test the sixteen different air filters, CU put each unit

in a sealed room and measured how much smoke and dust it could remove from the air over a thirty-minute test period. Of the sixteen units CU tested, the Ionic Breeze Quadra model came in dead last, since it managed "no measurable reduction in airborne particles."

Sharper Image was upset at the test results. "They said the Ionic Breeze needed to run longer," a CU attorney said. "So Consumer Reports went back and tested again, this time seeing how much cigarette smoke could be removed over nineteen hours. It couldn't even clean the smoke from one-eighth of a cigarette" in that time.

In late 2003, *Consumer Reports* again tested air filters, and the Quadra again ranked last in the rankings.

Not surprisingly, Sharper Image was once again upset. "They told Consumers Union again that the test was unfair," the attorney spokesman said. "So Consumers Union asked what test they'd like [us] to run. They have never, to this day, recommended a test for Consumers Union to do."

Sharper Image did, however, have a plan of action: It sued CU in U.S. District Court, alleging the articles in CU's magazine *Consumer Reports* were based on "bad test procedures" and constituted "negligent product disparagement."

But wait a minute: Aren't reviews part of what's covered by the First Amendment of the U.S. Constitution? Shouldn't a testing organization be allowed to publish its opinion as to what it thinks about a product, even if the manufacturer doesn't like what they say, based on that explicit right?

Of course the First Amendment applies. So might the lawsuit by Sharper Image be considered a way to shut up a critic on an issue that affects the public?

"Sharper Image could have just let it go without drawing more attention to *Consumer Report*'s articles, but they didn't," said attorney Steven Williams, who represented CU in the case. "I think they wanted to have a chilling effect on the media." And surely if Sharper Image prevailed, other reviewers would be "chilled"—they'd have to think long and hard about publishing a negative review, no matter how objective it was, when they might have to pay out millions of dollars in damages. "When you strike at the core of the First Amendment and sue someone to protect marketing," Williams continued, "that's not really a proper use of the courts."

Recall that twenty-three states have specifically made SLAPP suits illegal. California, where Sharper Image filed its suit, is one of them. Williams filed a motion to dismiss Sharper Image's lawsuit on the basis that it was prohibited under California's anti-SLAPP law. U.S. District Court Judge Maxine Chesney agreed that the suit was an attempt at squelching CU's First Amendment rights of free speech—the very definition of a SLAPP. She not only dismissed the suit, she awarded CU $400,000 in legal fees that it spent to fight off Sharper Image's action.

"The court finds Sharper Image has not provided sufficient evidence to support a finding that, under any of [their argued] theories, whether alone or in combination, it has a reasonable probability of establishing that any of the challenged statements are false," Chesney wrote in her decision.

Sharper Image's lawyer said the retailer was "very disappointed in this result" and threatened to appeal the ruling.

"Hopefully, going forward, companies will think twice about filing these types of suits," CU attorney Williams said afterward. "It's not in their interest to be attacking free speech." Nor, indeed, is it in the public's interest.

Still, even though CU won, other publications might be

chilled, Williams says. "Consumers Union may not have backed down, but how willing will magazines like *Good Housekeeping* be in the future to criticize products? How willing will newspapers be to do independent reviews? What this case was really about was the First Amendment and the right to free speech."

Consumers Union has been sued fifteen times over the reviews it has published in *Consumer Reports*, but it has never had to issue a retraction or pay any legal judgments.

Obviously, anti-SLAPP laws don't give publications free rein to say anything they want; they don't entitle them to lie about a product, for instance. But when they've been objective in testing, or only stated opinion, and are still sued, such laws give them the lever they need to defend themselves and recover their usually significant legal costs.

So the case is a victory for the First Amendment, but don't cheer yet: While twenty-three states have adopted anti-SLAPP laws, that leaves twenty-seven which haven't. SLAPPs are thus still a powerful tool that can be used to stifle free expression in many parts of the country, and that affects us all.

Sources:

* ✳ "Sharper Image Loses Suit Over Panned Product," *The Recorder,* 11 November 2004
* ✳ "Sharper Image Fogs Up," *San Francisco Chronicle,* 14 November 2004

SLAPP Unhappy

In addition to California, anti-SLAPP laws are on the books in twenty-three states: Delaware, Florida, Georgia, Hawaii, Indiana, Louisiana, Maine, Maryland, Massachusetts, Minnesota, Missouri, Nebraska, Nevada, New Mexico, New York, Oklahoma, Oregon, Pennsylvania, Rhode Island, Tennessee, Utah, Washington, and West Virginia. (*Source: California Anti-SLAPP Project*)

1	*	) Location: California
2	Corporate Toy Behemoth	) Year: 2002
3	v.	) Award Status:
4	Corporate Music	) Dishonorable Mention
5	Behemoth	)

FREE SPEECH V. WORDS RESERVED FOR EXCLUSIVE CORPORATE USE

In 1997, MCA Records released the song "Barbie Girl" by the Danish group Aqua. To the dismay of Mattel, Inc., owner of the cash cow Barbie doll (and its registered trademark), the song quickly became a smash hit, both in the U.S. and abroad.

The lyrics were fairly banal, at least at the start: "Hiya Barbie! / Hi Ken! / You wanna go for a ride? / Sure, Ken! / Jump in! / Ha ha ha ha!" But the chorus—oh, the chorus: "I'm a Barbie girl, in my Barbie world / Life in plastic, it's fantastic / You can brush my hair, undress me everywhere / Imagination, life is your creation."

And then there were lines like, "I'm a blonde bimbo girl, in a fantasy world / Dress me up, make it tight, I'm your dolly," "Kiss me here, touch me there, hanky-panky," and "You can touch, you can play / You can say 'I'm always yours.' "

It didn't help that the song's catchy tune made it easy for young girls to memorize every word.

Mattel was not amused: It filed a federal lawsuit charging trademark infringement. Mattel argued the song would "create a likelihood of confusion in consumers," a standard claim in any trademark infringement case, and that the song "diluted" Mattel's Barbie trademark by "diminishing the trademark's capacity to identify the Mattel doll" and by "tarnishing the doll's good name, and thus the trademark, with risqué lyrics that were inappropriate" for the target market—young girls.

Trademarks are important: They tell consumers that a product comes from a particular source; misleading consumers into thinking that another product was produced by the trademark holder is infringement, unfair trade, and dilution (which courts define as the "whittling away of the value of a trademark").

To guard against such claims, MCA had included a disclaimer on the release that noted the song was "social commentary not created or approved by the makers of the doll." But such a disclaimer was "unacceptable," a Mattel spokesman told reporters. "It's akin to a bank robber handing a note of apology to a teller during a heist, [which] neither diminishes the severity of the crime, nor does it make it legal." He said the "Barbie Girl" song lyrics thus constituted "theft of another company's property."

MCA didn't take that legal maneuver lying down. "Bank robber"? it bristled. "Heist"? "Crime"? "Theft"? Them's fighting words. MCA filed a countersuit claiming libel.

In hearing the case, the Federal District Court ruled that the song indeed "diluted" Mattel's Barbie trademark, but pointed out there are three legal exclusions that allow such dilution: comparative advertising, news reporting, and commentary and noncommercial use. "MCA used Barbie's name to sell copies of the song," it ruled, but it was "noncommercial" because the song was clearly "social commentary on Barbie's image and the cultural values she represents." In other words, the song was parody and commentary, as allowed by the Constitution's free speech guarantee in the Bill of Rights.

"Parody and satire have to be excluded" from trademark dilution statutes, said Florida trademark attorney Mark Stein, commenting on the case. Otherwise, the entire Federal Trademark Dilution Act would be declared unconstitutional on First Amendment grounds.

"The parties are advised to chill," scolded Judge Alex Kozinski of the U.S. Court of Appeals, which unanimously upheld the decisions of the circuit court in throwing out both Mattel's trademark infringement claim and MCA's libel claim. "Simply put, the trademark owner does not have the right to control public discourse whenever the public imbues his mark with a meaning beyond its source-identifying function." Judge Kozinski pointed out that Barbie was originally modeled on a "German street walker" that Mattel turned into a "glamorous, long-legged blonde" that has been called both "the ideal American woman and a bimbo"—and that "with fame often comes unwanted attention."

"The song pokes fun at Barbie and the values that Aqua contends she represents," Judge Kozinski wrote in his opinion. Speech that "does more than propose a commercial transaction" is "entitled to full First Amendment protection."

Mattel might have been proud that they could turn a doll inspired by a foreign prostitute into an American icon that artists *want* to talk about. Instead, they sued over an obvious parody and got the only reward rightfully theirs: a Stella Award.

Total elapsed time in this case: five years.

Sources:

* "MCA Records Wins Barbie Battle," *National Law Journal*, 6 August 2002.
* "Mattel v. MCA Records, et al," U.S. Court of Appeal for the Ninth Circuit Opinion No. 98-56453, 24 July 2002

Afterword:

Several readers wrote in shock (*shock*, I tells ya!) at the judge's comment that Barbie "was originally modeled on a 'German street walker.'" But yes, dear readers who grew up in the sixties and later and are now mothers yourselves, your (and your little girl's) favorite doll was indeed inspired by a German doll for *men* called "Lilli." The original Barbie even was dressed similarly to Lilli—Barbie's "inventor," Ruth Handler, had picked up several of the dolls in Germany in 1957 and brought them to fellow Mattel founders to try to convince them that such a doll would have a market here. (It did: It's estimated that 172,000 Barbies sell *per day*. So now you know why Mattel would do *anything* to quickly plug any leaks in that cash geyser!)

Lilli (the doll) was modeled after a cartoon character in *Bild Zeitung*, a German newspaper. As *Salon* magazine put it in a 1997 feature, "A professional floozy of the first order, *Bild Zeitung*'s Lilli traded sex for money, delivered sassy comebacks to police officers, and sought the company of 'balding, jowly fatcats.' . . . While the cartoon Lilli was a user of men, the doll (who came into existence in

1955) was herself a plaything—a masculine joke, perhaps, for West German males who could not afford to play with a real Lilli. A German brochure from the 1950s confided that Lilli (the doll) was 'always discreet,' while her complete wardrobe made her 'the star of every bar.' "

Source:

* "The Littlest Harlot," *Salon,* November 1997

Barbie Redux

Mattel's humiliating defeat in the MCA case turned into a one-two punch. In another parody case, Mattel pursued Utah artist and photographer Tom Forsythe in court. He had created a photographic exhibit showing a Barbie doll "sometimes posed provocatively" with household appliances. Forsythe said he was trying to portray " 'crass consumerism,' and to me, that's Barbie." Mattel sued him in the U.S. District Court in Los Angeles, but the judge threw it out. Both sides appealed: Mattel because it wanted to stop Forsythe, and Forsythe because he wanted reimbursement of his legal fees after his win.

Forsythe won again; the Ninth Circuit Court of Appeals sent the case back to the District Court, suggesting that the judge should consider sanctions against Mattel. Judge Ronald S. W. Lew accepted the case back and awarded Forsythe more than $1.8 million, the legal equivalent of a clue-by-four between the toy-maker's corporate eyes.

The Barbie doll is an American institution, which makes it worthy of comment—which certainly includes parody, a point Judge Lew made very, very clear. "Plaintiff had access to sophisticated counsel who could have determined that such a suit was objectively unreasonable and frivolous," he ruled. "Instead it appears plaintiff forced defendant into costly litigation to discourage him from using Barbie's image in his artwork. This is just the sort of situation in which this court should award attorneys' fees to deter this type of litigation which contravenes the intent of the Copyright Act." Mattel would be foolish to appeal, since it would have to do so to the Ninth Circuit—the very court that suggested the sanctions.

(*Source: "Judge Says Artist Can Make Fun of Barbie,"* New York Times, *28 June 2004*)

```
1                    *              )  Location: Texas
2        Corporate Financial       )  Year: 2004
                                    )
3           Behemoth                )  Award Status: Runner-up
                                    )  for the 2004 Stella Award
4              v.                   )
                                    )
5         Crime Victim              )
```

WE'VE GOT YOUR
(ACCOUNT) NUMBER,
CHUMP

Robert and Suzanne Korinke faced the New American Nightmare: They were the victims of identity theft. In April 2001, the Korinkes went to refinance their mortgage and discovered someone had tapped into their homeowner's line of credit with Homecomings Financial in Texas. They had paid off their line of credit the year before and thought they had closed the account, but it had been run back up to $142,000. They had no idea the account was active again until they saw their credit report during the refinance procedure.

After spending countless hours to straighten out the mess, Homecomings Financial, a subsidiary of GMAC Financial Services, which is a division of General Motors, admitted in writing that the debt was fraudulent and the Korinkes, relieved, put the issue out of their minds.

Two years later, the Korinkes faced the other American Nightmare: They were being sued. As they sat down for

Christmas dinner, a messenger arrived with an "urgent package": notice of a lawsuit filed against them by Homecomings Financial.

The suit claimed the Korinkes were negligent in not informing the finance company of the fraud sooner and that "caused the injury to Homecomings," the lawsuit claimed. "As such, Korinke is liable for any and all sums attributed to his negligence." It demanded about $74,000 plus attorneys' fees.

Naturally, the Korinkes didn't notify Homecomings about the fraud right away because they didn't know about it themselves—the company had accepted a change-of-address form from the crooks so the Korinkes wouldn't get the bills from the company, and sent a new checkbook to the new address by overnight mail. The fraudulent address change was, indeed, part of what the Korinkes had cleared up in 2001—the company admitted it hadn't sent any notice to the old address, which would have allowed the couple to detect the fraud earlier. But the company did send a notice to the fraudsters to inform them that the address was changed back.

"I was outraged when I heard about this," said attorney Mari J. Frank, an identity theft expert who is defending the couple. In a remarkable example of stopping a frivolous suit in its tracks, Frank was able to get the company to drop the suit just a month after it was filed. Homecomings even announced it "regrets the inconvenience this incident has caused the Korinkes." It also noted, "We are actively working to resolve this issue fairly." As if it were "fair" in the first place to sue the victims of a crime it helped occur?

On the other hand, the suit was dropped "without prejudice," meaning the company has the right to file it again.

Homecomings's attorney, J. Allan Smith, refused to discuss the suit or why it wasn't dropped "with prejudice." Afraid to put the matter out of their minds—since that hadn't worked before—the couple is understandably nervous that they're still not in the clear. Meanwhile, they've spent about $5,000 in legal bills to clear up the matter.

"How does Joe Consumer fight a big bank?" asked Linda Foley, the founder of the Identity Theft Resource Center in San Diego. "If you come out whole, you should consider yourself really lucky."

Despite the Identity Theft and Assumption Deterrence Act of 1998, which made identity theft a federal crime, it's a huge and growing criminal activity with an estimated seven million U.S. victims in 2002. Financial institutions must be more proactive to ensure it doesn't happen—prevention is much better than after-the-fact law enforcement. Instead, and as this case illustrates, financial institutions can, and sometimes do, take outrageous actions against innocent customers, claiming that the victims of crimes are responsible for losses that are out of their control, making them victims all over again.

The Korinkes are indeed "really lucky" that they were able to find an attorney who specializes in the exact sort of case they were involved in and was able to get the suit dropped quickly. But even then, it was at a substantial cost of time and money. Stress, hours of work, and thousands of dollars is "lucky"? In the world of frivolous lawsuits, it very sadly is.

Sources:

* "ID Theft Victims Face Tough Bank Fights," MSNBC, 18 February 2004

* "Loan Firm's Customers Sing Chorus of Gripes," *San Jose Mercury News,* 7 March 2004

The Political Divide

As noted, Republicans tend to favor tort reform, in theory because it's "pro-business," while Democrats oppose tort reform, in theory because it favors business over downtrodden individuals.

A look at the political contributions by the Association of Trial Lawyers of America, whose members initiate most civil suits, shows the divide. In the 2002 election cycle, ATLA made $4,246,088 in political contributions. All but $348,685 of that total went to Democrats.

(*Source: Center for Responsive Politics*)

```
1              *            )  Location: New York
2  Corporate Book Behemoth  )  Year: 2003
                            )
3             v.            )  Award Status:
4    Corporate Newspaper    )  Dishonorable Mention
                            )
5         Behemoth          )
                            )
```

HARRY POTTER AND THE
COLOSSAL LAWSUIT

The Harry Potter book series is a smash. Author J. K. Rowling has gone from a single mother on welfare to the richest woman in the United Kingdom. By June 2003 the first four books had sales of over 203 million copies.

The books' American publisher, Scholastic Inc., was so confident in the potential of book five, *Harry Potter and the Order of the Phoenix,* it ordered an initial print run of an "unprecedented" 8.5 million copies. It also worked up a $3 million to $4 million publicity campaign to ensure huge quantities could be sold in a frenzy of adolescent hype.

Unlike with many "big" books, Scholastic decided not to send out prepublication review copies. Bookstores were told they could not sell any copies until one minute after midnight on June 21, ensuring huge lineups at the stores that were open—a perfect "photo opportunity" of anxious buyers to play into the massive publicity campaign.

In short, the publisher hoped to get total control over

every bit of publicity being splashed out in every media outlet possible. It went off almost perfectly, but the key word there is "almost."

A health food store in New York City that has a small book section received four copies of the book. The owner says no one told him that he had to wait until June 21 to sell them, so he put them in his window. Is it plausible that he was not warned? Yes: A full case of books was ten copies, and the embargo warning was included on a sticker on the box. But he only got four, so it's entirely possible that the distributor packed them in a different box without a sticker, meaning the store owner may not have ever been given legal notice of the embargo.

In any case, a *New York Daily News* reporter, seeing the books for sale and realizing the obvious scoop potential, bought one of the health store's books. On June 18, three days before the book's worldwide release, the *Daily News* ran a review, along with a brief synopsis of the plot after warning, "If you don't want to know anything about how Harry and his pals spend their fifth year at the Hogwarts School of Witchcraft and Wizardry, stop now and buy the book when it's officially released Saturday." The article was illustrated by a photo of the open book, showing two of its eight hundred pages.

Unfair! cried Scholastic, since a tiny aspect of its carefully orchestrated campaign was thwarted. The publisher and author immediately—the very day that the newspaper was published—filed suit in United States District Court in New York claiming the newspaper's "blatant and willful violation" damaged "Rowling's valuable intellectual property rights." Why would they do such a dastardly thing? Surely it's not to inform the public on a story of very obvious interest, but rather it's because the newspaper "seek[s] to deprive Rowling of her right and ability to control" her work. Those actions "have irreparably harmed the carefully orchestrated, multimillion-dollar marketing plans" the publisher made.

Continuing on, the lawsuit says, "Scholastic and Rowling have worked hard to ensure that [the book's] plot details and character development remain secret until the book's official release"—conveniently leaving out the fact that Rowling had already leaked a blockbuster tidbit to the press: that a major character is "killed off" in the book. They charge that the newspaper's "willful violation of the release embargo" somehow ruined their effort to keep everything "a surprise for eager fans to discover as quickly as they turn the book's pages."

For this, the lawsuit says, Rowling and Scholastic are "entitled" to $100 million in damages, plus "all gains, profits, and advantages" the newspaper derived from its "unlawful" actions.

The embargo isn't a legally binding contract on anyone who does not agree to it. Bookstores that wanted to sell the book apparently were happy to make such an agreement. The newspaper, however, was not a party to it. For Scholastic and author J. K. Rowling to insist that it must comply with its marketing scheme isn't reasonable, making the suit against the paper ridiculous. If they have a valid beef, it's with the store that sold the book—and they have a plausible defense. What the little store doesn't have is a plausibly deep pocket.

Scholastic was happy to get huge publicity in newspapers, but when it can't control the content of one publication that was certainly not a party to its "embargo," they whine that the surprise is somehow ruined for readers the world over, because the article was not just in its newspaper, but also on its Web site.

"We will vigorously defend any action and are confident we did nothing wrong journalistically or legally," said a *Daily News* spokesman.

Scholastic bet $3 million they could control what every bookstore, newspaper, magazine, and Web site in the country could say, and when, about the new Harry Potter book—a country that guarantees freedom of speech and freedom of the press. They lost that bet. To think that creating such a plan, and spending millions to support it, entitles them to damages when a free press dares to print a review contrary to their schedule shows an incredible arrogance—as does their abuse of the civil court system to go thirty-three times or nothing on their cynical bet.

Sources:

* Multiple news sources, including "Harry Potter Publisher Sues NY Newspaper," Reuters, 18 June 2003
* "J. K. Rowling and Scholastic Inc., v. *New York Daily News*," Lawsuit filing, 18 June 2003

Afterword:

Plenty of Harry Potter fans complained about this case. One noted that "Scholastic spent $3 million in an effort to coordinate the release of a book, sales of which are largely dependent on the suspense of the fans. The author and publisher made sure that everybody knew that nobody was to read the book before June 21st, and the courts should decide whether or not they should have that power. What possible purpose could be served by printing the review on June 18th rather than June 21st? It was a pointless publicity stunt that real newspapers should be above, and I hope it blows up in their faces. And I have to say, you seem to have a negative opinion toward the huge success this book achieved. Whether or not you enjoy the books, there are untold millions of fans earned by the author's previous books, and there is no reason the next book should not have massive sales. Rowling has earned it."

Rowling definitely *has* earned her place in publishing (and financial) history. She created a terrific premise and cast of characters and deserves her riches. So why doesn't the newspaper also have the right to make money? "What possible purpose" did the newspaper have to print the review before the embargo? *To make money,* of course! That's what they're in business to do. Several readers also suggested that, while Scholastic and Rowling were "right" to sue, the amount was "excessive" and should be donated to charity. If they're right—if their business and profits were damaged—why in the world should they give any winnings to charity? The readers' discomfort over the amount is telling: They *don't* think it's right that Rowling and Scholastic should profit from the supposed "damage." So if they don't deserve monetary damages, small or large, why do they deserve to sue?

A number of readers also objected to the newspaper "ruining the surprise" by publishing a plot summary. People who didn't want the "surprise" revealed to them shouldn't have read the story! As noted, the paper warned readers to "stop now"—and encouraged them to "buy the book when it's officially released Saturday." Once the book was published, did sales suddenly stop because the people who bought it the first day knew what the plot was? Obviously not. Unsurprisingly, the book topped the *New York Times'* Children's Hardcover Best Seller list for a long run—and at the same time Best Sellers two through five were other Harry Potter titles, despite their "surprises" being "ruined" long before. Meanwhile, three months after filing the case, Scholastic and Rowling quietly dropped it.

```
1              *           )   Location: Wisconsin
2     Pedophile Priest     )   Year: 2003
                           )
3           v.             )   Award Status: Runner-up
                           )   for the 2003 Stella Award
4        His Victim        )
5   ------------------------ )
```

SLAPP HIM AROUND

With the recent barrage of press coverage, you might think lawsuits against the Roman Catholic Church over priests molesting children in their flock are something new. They're not. In 1990, John Ramstack received $65,000 to settle a case against Father David Hanser, now 70 and retired. The charges were tough to ponder: Ramstack and three brothers say Hanser molested them over a period of years at his lake cottage in Merton, Wisconsin.

The out-of-court settlement agreement, which was also signed by the Archdiocese of Milwaukee, required that the Ramstack brothers stay silent about their case—they couldn't go public when the more recent allegations surfaced in cities across the nation. On the other side of the coin, Father Hanser agreed not to work or volunteer near children.

After the more recent scores of cases stretching from Boston to Los Angeles came to light and put the church in crisis, the Ramstacks say they learned Father Hanser was still working near children, as a chaplain at several hospitals. They say they called a church bishop to complain, but their call was ignored. Since they figure Hanser had broken his part of the agreement, the Ramstack brothers went public against him, hoping to prevent the abuse of other children. They gave an interview to the *Milwaukee Journal Sentinel* about the years of abuse they suffered at the hands of a man who was supposed to be giving them spiritual and moral guidance. They also sued Hanser for breach of contract—for working near children despite their settlement agreement.

"It's up to the Church to decide where he works," said John Schiro, Hanser's attorney, denying that the priest had broken the secret agreement. He said if the Ramstacks had a problem with Hanser's actions, they should have complained to the archdiocese. What about the ignored phone call? "I'm not aware that they ever complained to anybody" other than the newspaper, he said. The Ramstacks were the ones guilty of breaking the agreement, he said, by suing for breach of contract, since that revealed the charges against Hanser.

In return, Father Hanser has sued John Ramstack for revealing the contents of their secret agreement. The suit asks for the return of the $65,000 paid in the 1990 settlement and a dismissal of the Ramstacks' case.

The Ramstacks' attorney, Timothy Clark, said barring the Ramstacks from suing Hanser for working near children is "against public policy, if not unconscionable." Further, he noted, after the nationwide molestation scandal broke, the Archdiocese of Milwaukee "publicly stated that they will not enforce any of these [confidentiality] agreements" that Hanser is asking the court to enforce. Indeed, the Church does not back Hanser on his countercomplaint: "The Archdiocese does not encourage or support countersuits by priests," said Kathleen Hohl, Archdiocese of Milwaukee communications coordinator, but she added they cannot control what priests do "as individuals."

But Waukesha County Circuit Judge J. Mac Davis said it may be necessary that the archdiocese explain the terms of the secret settlement, since it signed the agreement—bringing it into the middle of the dueling lawsuits, even though both Ramstack and Hanser want the archdiocese to keep out of things. When the story broke, Hanser retired from his hospital work, and the archdiocese ordered him to refrain from conducting any ministry.

It is unconscionable for anyone responsible for the well-being of children to abuse that trust, especially sexually. It is a disgrace for that person to be allowed to sweep his crimes under the rug and be given a new assignment where he can start his abuse anew on fresh victims. When caught, penitence is in order, not a lawsuit that tries to slap down the accuser and, by extension, put other victims on notice that they better keep their mouths shut, too, or else. It is time for pedophiles—church-based and otherwise—to be brought to justice, not for them to abuse the courts in an attempt to force their victims to remain silent.

Sources:

* "Priest in Abuse Case Sues His Accuser," *Milwaukee Journal Sentinel,* 20 December 2002
* "Judge Calls on Church to Explain Settlement," *Milwaukee Journal Sentinel,* 7 January 2003

1	*	)	Location: Connecticut
2	Huge Newspaper Chain	)	Year: 2004
3	v.	)	Award Status: Runner-up
4	Newspaper Carrier	)	for the 2004 Stella Award
5		)	

PAYDAY PLAY

Mark Guthrie, 43, is a former newspaper carrier for the *Hartford Courant* of Connecticut, which is owned by the Tribune Company of Chicago. There is also a baseball player by the name of Mark Guthrie, who is five years younger than the carrier; he formerly played for the Chicago Cubs, which is also owned by the Tribune Company.

In 2003, the Tribune Company's payroll department mixed the two men up and deposited $301,000 of the baseball player's pay into the newspaper carrier's bank account. It took five weeks for the company to detect the error. The low-paid deliveryman noticed the money, but didn't touch it out of fear—he knew it was a mistake, and cooperated with Tribune when the baseball pitcher wanted his misplaced salary.

But Guthrie of Connecticut stopped the last $26,000 from being taken out of his account until the company proved to him that he would not suffer any tax ramifications over the company's error. "I need them to open the books to me and show me I don't have any tax liabilities," he said. "It's mind-boggling. They never should have made the mistake to begin with." Plus, he says, he thinks his own pay was given to the baseball player. All he wants, he says, is a full accounting so he knows he was paid correctly and won't suffer financially from the company's mistake.

Tribune, not about to be jerked around by one of its newsboys, balked. In 2004, rather than provide the accounting the carrier so reasonably asked for, the company sued him, demanding the return of the rest of the money. "We have no desire to embarrass Mr. Guthrie or bring undue attention to his actions," said Cubs attorney Paul Guggina. "We just want the money back." The Connecticut Guthrie has hired his own lawyer, and now says he won't settle until Tribune pays for that expense, too.

Guthrie the baseball player didn't get picked up by the Cubs and is now a free agent. Guthrie the newspaper carrier was also dropped by the media conglomerate due to the lawsuit—and is presumably also now a free agent.

Source:

* "Payments Spawn Lawsuit; Tribune Sues Ex-Worker, Seeking Misdirected Money," *Hartford Courant*, 10 September 2004

```
1              *            )  Location: Mississippi
                            )
2      The Uninvolved       )  Year: 2003
                            )
3           v.              )  Award Status:
                            )  Dishonorable Mention
4      The Innocent         )
                            )
5  ------------------------  )
```

MOBIUS LOGIC

The state of Mississippi is well known as a place where sympathetic juries provide huge payouts to plaintiffs [See, for example, "Unwanted Side Effects," page 183]. To illustrate this point, CBS TV's *60 Minutes* aired a segment on lawsuits in Mississippi's Jefferson County, and quoted a local man who said jurors gave out money "because they felt as if they were going to get a cut off of it."

Morley Safer, the *60 Minutes* correspondent, wanted to be sure he heard that right: "The jurors benefit? Is that what you're saying?" he asked.

"They benefit after court, and everything is over with. Yes, sir," he replied, adding it was "under the table."

The local man did not identify any specific juror or any particular case, but two of the thousands of people who have sat on Jefferson County juries objected to the characterization. Anthony Berry, who was on a jury that awarded a $150 million verdict in an asbestos case, and Johnny Anderson, who was on a panel that awarded $150 million in a diet drug case, have filed suit—in Jefferson County, of course—against CBS and a newspaper publisher who made similar comments on the broadcast. They say the comments "were libelous, slanderous and defamatory" against Jefferson County juries as a whole and are seeking $597 million in "actual" damages and $5.9 billion in punitive damages.

"This suit proves the truthfulness of what I said on TV," said publisher Wyatt Emmerich. "If you can expand slander to include an entire class, there is no free speech," he said. "You can't say anything critical."

And that's exactly what many lawsuits are designed to do: strike fear into commentators so they will stop public discussion of problems so the people causing the problems in the first place can continue on, without anyone looking over their shoulders.

Source:

* "TV Show on Mississippi Justice Stirs Suit," *Jackson Clarion-Ledger,* 10 December 2002

 ## Mess in Mississippi

When the class-action lawsuit against the diet drug fen-phen was in full swing, there was a rash of prescription forgery cases in Jackson County, Mississippi. Drug addicts trying to get a fix? Nope: People were forging scrips for fen-phen so they could get in on the multihundred-million-dollar lawsuit! Twelve people have been convicted so far, and more arrests are pending thanks to an FBI investigation. Each of the dirty dozen allegedly received $250,000 for being a part of the settlement as "victims" of the drug combo—less about $100,000 each for attorneys' fees. (*Source:* Jackson Clarion-Ledger)

```
1              *            )  Location: California
                            )
2        Big Tobacco        )  Year: 2003
                            )
3            v.             )  Award Status:
                            )  Dishonorable Mention
4  Anti-Smoking Lobbyists   )
                            )
5  ------------------------ )
```

IT COULDN'T HAVE HAPPENED TO A NICER INDUSTRY

Tobacco companies have long been the bogeymen of U.S. industry. It was proven that they manipulated nicotine levels and lied about the safety of their product, leading to hundreds of thousands, if not millions, of deaths in the U.S. alone. Long pounded in the courts, "big tobacco" finally lost big time with a multibillion-dollar "settlement" to be paid to each of the fifty states to compensate the states for caring for indigent tobacco victims and to help educate their citizens as to the dangers of smoking.

No state has been more active in anti-smoking public awareness campaigns than California, which started anti-tobacco advertising long before the settlement in a bold attempt to convince smokers to stop, and nonsmokers not to start. The ads are funded by a 25-cent-per-pack tax on cigarettes voters approved in 1988. In the ads, the state likes to say that it's "America's smoke-free section," and apparently the campaign is working: Since the special tax passed, cigarette sales have dropped by half in California.

R. J. Reynolds spokeswoman Ellen Matthews says that the decade-long ad effort in California has "infiltrated every segment of the media in California." Well, yeah: That was pretty much the state's goal. But, RJR says, that result has prejudiced potential jurors in any future anti-tobacco court action in the state against them—so much so that the tobacco companies are "vilified" by the people who may have to judge them in hypothetical future lawsuits.

Thus, R. J. Reynolds and Lorillard, two of the largest to-bacco companies in the U.S., have sued California in federal court in Sacramento, asking the court to order a stop to the state's anti-tobacco advertising.

"Suing to stop the most successful tobacco prevention program in the nation is further proof that they're not serious in saying they don't want kids to smoke," said Bill Corr, executive director of the Campaign for Tobacco-Free Kids in Washington, D.C.

California's then-governor, Gray Davis, said he was ready for the fight the companies have picked. "I say, bring it on," Davis said. "They spend infinitely more than we do [on marketing] to get their message out. I don't think anyone should feel too sorry for them."

Tobacco companies "vilified"? The horror! But it's hardly surprising that an industry so often sued would think of using the courts to get what it wants. As in love and war, the tobacco business thinks turnabout is fair play.

If the government cannot warn citizens about a product *known* and even *proven* to be harmful to health, how would it possibly be able to warn us about products that *probably* or *might* have health implications? Is it really in society's best interests for such information to be suppressed?

Source:

* "Tobacco Companies Sue State, Saying Ads 'Vilify' Industry," Associated Press, 2 April 2003

```
1              *             )  Location: Washington
2        Penny Pincher       )  Year: 2003
                             )
3             v.             )  Award Status:
                             )  Dishonorable Mention
4        Party Hostess       )
                             )
5  -------------------------- )
```

GIVE THEM A PENNY AND THEY'LL WANT A DOLLAR

Wendy Ehringer of Seattle took some friends out for burgers. Her $15.02 check to the restaurant bounced, so the restaurant turned the debt over to its collection agency.

When she got the notice from Associated Credit Service demanding the full amount plus $40 in fees, Ehringer said she thought, "I better take care of this," and mailed a money order to ACS for the full amount. She didn't think a thing more about it until several months later when she was notified she had been sued.

While ACS's lawsuit showed she had a balance of "$0.00," it claimed she was a day or two late in getting the money order to them. The suit was filed to get the interest on the supposedly late payment—18 cents.

"When I saw I was being sued for 18 cents, I was outraged," Ehringer said. In addition to the 18 cents, the collection agency was demanding $311.26 in attorneys' fees and other costs. It was war. "At that point, I knew there was no stopping this train," she said.

Ehringer, a paralegal, knew plenty of lawyers, so she asked one to help her. Attorney Amanda Lee sent a letter to ACS, but when the company ignored it Lee filed a countersuit. "Once they cashed that check, they didn't have any basis" to claim more fees, Lee said. "You can't file a lawsuit if you're not actually owed the money."

The collection agency wouldn't budge, and the case came before Judge Eileen Kato in Seattle District Court. Judge Kato ruled that ACS had violated the Consumer Protection Act and the Collection Agency Act, and threw out the 18-cent suit. She also ordered ACS to pay Ehringer $500 in damages, and ruled the collection agency would have to pay Ehringer's attorney for her time—a total of thirty-six hours' worth, Lee figures, for a total of over $7,000. A hearing was set to assess the exact total.

"The $500 in damages might not get their attention," Lee said. "But if they have to pay attorneys' fees, it might."

There are plenty of deadbeats out there, and collection agencies play an important role to keep innocent businesses from being victimized by them. But when a slimy agency tries to pull a fast one, they deserve to be slapped down. Hard. A tin-plated 18-cent Stella Award goes to ACS. And official Stella Kudos to Ehringer and Lee for fighting back, and to Judge Kato for upholding justice.

While not judged as a SLAPP case, it's a great example of how corporations attempt to bully people into submission by abusing the courts. (Note: The newspaper reporter who covered this story asked ACS's attorney, Paul Wasson, to explain the company's side of the case. He "declined to comment.")

Source:

* "Suit over 18 Cents Redefines 'Small-Claims' Court," *Seattle Times,* 26 September 2002

Your Turn
"Try" a Few Cases

After chapter upon chapter of cases, you should be getting the hang of things. So read the following cases and, where they pause, consider how you would vote if you were on the jury. Because in fact you are on the jury—in the Court of Public Opinion.

1	*	) Location: Missouri
2	Grieving Mother	) Year: 2004
3	v.	) Award Status: Runner-up
4	His Ride	) for the 2004 Stella Award
5		)

END RUN

Derrick Thomas of the Kansas City Chiefs football team was good. As a linebacker, he helped the team win plenty of games, and was well on his way to smashing various records. In his first year with the Chiefs, for instance, he sacked opposing quarterbacks ten times. In his second year, he doubled that number. When asked how he did it, he'd simply reply with a smile, "Speed kills."

As a person, he gave a lot back to his community. Chiefs president Carl Peterson remembers how Thomas would collect money each year for food drives for the needy. "He would go around the locker room and demand money from his teammates—at least $100, usually more," Peterson said. "Then he'd come into my office and say, 'What will the Chiefs do to match this?' We'd negotiate, because he loved to negotiate, and we'd decide on how much the Chiefs were going to give. And then he'd say, 'OK, Father, we know what the Chiefs are going to do. Now, what are you going to do?' "

Peterson calls Thomas "the son I never had."

A quick annual holiday fund-raiser wasn't all, of course. Thomas's father had been killed in Vietnam, so he knew the pain of being fatherless. He spent lots of time with kids, helping them learn how to read so that they, too, could break out of the inner city and get to a better life.

Once, during a game against Denver, Thomas got angry, "blowing up" during the game, and was suspended. Rather than blame others, he held a press conference and addressed "the youth of America who look up to Derrick Thomas" and urged them not to make the same mistake he did. The kind of role model sports stars should be, but often aren't.

In January 2000, Thomas was driving in his car, a large Chevy Suburban sport-utility, on Interstate 435 in a Kansas City snowstorm. There were ice patches on the road. Witnesses say he was driving too fast. Thomas lost control and rolled the SUV. His friend and assistant, Michael Tellis, was thrown out of the vehicle and killed. Thomas was also thrown out; he landed in oncoming traffic lanes and was left partly paralyzed. Neither had been wearing a seat belt; a third passenger in the backseat was wearing a seat belt and suffered only minor injuries.

In the hospital, Thomas was making progress toward recovery. Two weeks after the accident, however, a blood clot killed him. He was just 33.

"Damnit, D, you had it all, man," editorialized Topeka sportswriter Rick Dean. "If only you'd just slowed down a little!" Or had been wearing a seat belt.

Another good guy cut down in a senseless tragedy, perhaps complicated by risk-taking speeds and the lack of a seat belt. That's how everyone saw it. Everyone, that is, except his mother.

Edith Morgan, Thomas's mother, said her son died because his SUV's roof was not strong enough to take the weight of the massive vehicle when it rolled over. It collapsed eight to ten inches, breaking his neck, she said.

Morgan—on behalf of herself, Thomas's estate, and the five mothers of his seven children—sued General Motors, the SUV's manufacturer; the Metropolitan Ambulance Services Trust, the nonprofit ambulance company that tried to save his life; and Royal Chevrolet of Harrisonville, Missouri, the dealer that sold Thomas the vehicle.

The suit, filed in Jackson County Circuit Court by attorney Gary C. Robb, claims wrongful death. It says the vehicle's roof was defective and the ambulance workers were negligent. The dealer? Who knows what they did wrong by selling Thomas the vehicle he wanted?

During trial, several facts emerged:

* The Suburban's vehicle class exempts it from federal roof crush standards. However, Suburbans *exceeded* that standard anyway.

* Accident reconstruction experts testified that Thomas was thrown out of the vehicle's passenger window before the roof collapsed. He couldn't have been thrown out after it collapsed, they said, since the window opening would then have been too small for the linebacker to go through it.

* There was no blood or other evidence that Thomas's neck was broken inside the vehicle by the collapsed roof. Defense experts say Thomas broke his neck by tumbling along the highway for fifty feet after being thrown from the vehicle.

* A traffic engineer calculated that Thomas had been driving somewhere between sixty-three and seventy-three miles per hour when he lost control. The posted speed

limit was seventy but, again, Thomas was driving in a
snowstorm on icy roads. (Plaintiff's attorney Michael Piuze
countered that the expert he had hired said Thomas was
going at most fifty-eight miles per hour. As if that was a
safe speed in an icy snowstorm.)

Before the trial started, the nonprofit ambulance service settled for $100,000 and was dropped from the suit.
The Chevy dealer that sold the SUV also settled; the
amount it paid was not reported.

In closing arguments, Piuze, the family's trial attorney,
pleaded with the jurors to remember Thomas's charity
work. He reminded them of his children, asking, "What's
it like not to have a daddy?" Then, a reporter said, "almost
whispering to the jury," he urged the panel to award at
least $75 million, perhaps more than $100 million, in
damages, avoiding a top figure because he "did not want
to put an upper limit on it."

Piuze is a bit of a specialist in rollover crash cases, having taken four of them to trial, three against GM. He won
every one of them.

In response, General Motors' attorney John Hickey
urged the jurors to consider personal responsibility.
Thomas was going too fast and wasn't wearing a seat belt.
Evidence showed his neck was not broken by the collapsed roof—the roof that actually exceeded federal standards, even though it was not required to even meet them.
"General Motors did absolutely nothing wrong," he said.
Rather, Thomas "was driving faster than anyone else on
the road and cutting in and out of traffic," even in the face
of worsening road conditions.

With that, the jurors started their deliberations.

There's the evidence. So how would you, as a member

of the Court of Public Opinion, rule in the case? You can find either side 100 percent at fault, or assign a percentage of the blame to General Motors.

After deliberating for five hours over two days, the jury found Thomas was entirely at fault, not even finding GM partially responsible for his injuries and resulting death. The vote was ten to two against his mother, Edith Morgan. (Missouri's constitution requires a two-thirds majority of the jury to decide civil trials, rather than a unanimous verdict.)

"The quality of the car made the jury open to what happened and maybe helped them put Thomas's celebrity status aside," said Hickey.

"I'm disappointed, because I felt so strongly about the rollovers," Morgan said. She said she would continue to press for improved roof strength standards.

Piuze said pretrial publicity was at least in part to blame for the failed suit, in that many of the articles about Thomas's death noted he was driving too fast and not wearing a seat belt. He said the message of the case is: Wear seat belts.

Not even close: The message delivered loud and clear by the jury is that people need to be held responsible for their own actions, and they—or their survivors—don't deserve nine-figure windfalls when they drive like idiots, even if they are normally very nice people who work hard to help others. Thomas killed himself accidentally—and, not incidentally, he killed his friend. Why should General

Motors be responsible for that? The obvious answer: They shouldn't.

Meanwhile, consider the ambulance company, which surely did nothing wrong. It either had to cough up $100,000 plus legal expenses or its insurance company did. Who can blame them for not wanting to take the risk that a sympathetic jury would sock it to them in a case of a fallen hometown hero? But no matter who paid its gigantic bill to get dropped from the case, the nonprofit organization certainly suffered a setback in its efforts to serve the citizens in and around Kansas City.

Thomas's death is a sad waste of his potential, both as a ballplayer and as a human being. And the greedy struggle to hold someone else responsible for his actions was a similar, sad waste.

Total elapsed time from accident to the conclusion of his mother's case: four and a half years.

Sources:

* "Days of Testimony Detail Seconds of Fatal Crash," *Kansas City Star,* 12 August 2004
* "Jury Deliberates Thomas Lawsuit," *Kansas City Star,* 17 August 2004
* "GM Prevails in Thomas Family Suit," *Kansas City Star,* 18 August 2004
* Various background articles from the "Chiefs Zone" Web site (chiefszone.cjonline.com), produced by the *Topeka Capital-Journal* newspaper

```
1                *            )  Location: Montana
                              )
2          Jack Ass          )  Year: 2002
                              )
3              v.            )  Award Status: Runner-up
                              )  for the 2002 Stella Award
4          Jackass          )
                              )
5  ---------------------------)
```

IF THE NAME FITS . . .

In 1997 Bob Craft, then 39, of Hot Springs, Montana, went to court to change his name. The Sanders County District Court approved it, and from then on Craft went by his memorable new, preferred name: Jack Ass.

Three years later, MTV's TV show *Jackass* went on the air, featuring the kind of crude jokes and dumb stunts that adolescent males of all ages seem to lap up with a spoon. Some morons have tried to copy the stunts, or film themselves doing other dumb tricks that they hope to impress the producers with. When they get hurt, they often sue.

But Jack Ass isn't . . . um . . . that sort of jackass. He isn't interested in doing stupid stunts; when he wasn't working as a freelance telephone and electric power lineman, he represented his "Hearts Across America" organization to campaign for responsible drinking and the use of designated drivers using the slogan, "Be a smart ass, not a dumb ass."

After seven years, Ass said he spent as much as $100,000 promoting his safe drinking message, against a total income of $1,500.

Apparently MTV's *Jackass* series and movie were getting in the way of that incredible cash flow. Ass thus filed a lawsuit that claims that the TV show promoting irresponsible behavior was somehow "plagiarized" from his efforts to promote responsible behavior, that the show infringes his trademarks and copyrights, and that this has demeaned, denigrated, and damaged his public service efforts.

"For over two years I have searched for an attorney with some courage to go up against MTV for the infringement and plagiarizing they have done," he said, but he couldn't and gave up—and thus filed the suit on his own against Viacom, which owns both MTV and Paramount Pictures, which distributes *Jackass: The Movie*.

"I have been working on these endeavors for more than seven years and I have put everything I had and a whole bunch I didn't have into this," Ass said. "Financially, mentally and physically I have paid heavily in all of these areas. I have lived in my car for over a year and went months being homeless to help fund this work," he added. "I intend that this will get some major media attention, thereby also attracting an attorney for representation. The *Jackass* movie has brought in over $50 million and I intend for the majority of those funds to go to Hearts Across America."

If nothing else, Ass has shown one thing, perhaps to the detriment of his own case: There are a lot of jackasses in the U.S.A.

But enough of the prejudice-inducing jokes. You've got the basics of the case, so how do you think the court ruled?

In January 2003, Viacom got the case moved to federal court, which is proper for both copyright and trademark cases—Ass erred by filing it in state court. Within a few months, the federal judge dismissed the suit. Shortly after, in July 2003, decidedly dissatisfied with the "major media attention" he had sought, Ass wrote out his own eulogy and then shot himself in the head with a hunting rifle. He was 45. Elapsed time from the alleged injury to being thrown out of court: about three years.

Sources:

* " 'Jackass'—the Lawsuit," *Missoulian,* 6 December 2002
* "Hot Springs Man Who Changed Name to Jack Ass Dies," *Missoulian,* 1 August 2003

```
1              *              )   Location: Michigan
                              )
2          Gambler           )   Year: 2003
                              )
3            v.               )   Award Status:
                              )   Dishonorable Mention
4          Casino            )
                              )
5   ------------------------- )
```

AIN'T WORTH A
PLUGGED NICKEL

Estella Romanski of Troy, Michigan, spotted a nickel in the tray of an unattended slot machine at the MotorCity Casino in Detroit. She picked up the coin and tried to play it, but a security guard stopped her—the rules of most casinos state that gamers can't touch winnings that don't belong to them unless they find them on the floor.

The security guard and the 73-year-old woman differ on what happened next, but Romanski claims she was "humiliated" by being asked to leave the casino over 5 cents and filed suit in Wayne County Circuit Court, asking for $100,000 for violations of her "civil rights." A mediation panel recommended that the casino pay Romanski $17,009.05 (the nickel, plus the $9 Romanski paid for her bus ticket to the casino, plus $17,000 for "humiliation and aggravation"). But both sides rejected the settlement and the casino has successfully moved the case to federal court.

Um, a constitutional right to violate house rules? Well, it's a theory. . . .

OK, those are the basics: How would you decide this case?

Romanski won: A federal jury awarded her \$875,000. "We hope they fix things and stop using gestapo tactics," one juror said, adding that some jurors thought the \$875,000 wasn't enough.

The casino is considering an appeal. It took twenty-three months to go from incident to the conclusion of the federal trial.

Sources:

* "Civil Rights Case in Federal Court: All Bets Are Off," *Detroit Free Press,* 26 September 2002
* "Troy Woman Gets \$875,000 in Casino Case," *Detroit Free Press,* July 23, 2003

```
1              *              )   Location: Massachusetts
                              )
2          Gambler           )   Year: 2004
                              )
3             v.              )   Award Status:
                              )   Dishonorable Mention
4           State            )
                              )
5  ------------------------------)
```

I WANT IT ALL, AND I WANT IT NOW

Louise Outing of Everett, Massachusetts, is 94 years old, but she's still pretty sharp. She even likes playing the lottery. And on September 4, 2004, she won $5.6 million in the Megabucks lottery drawing.

Massachusetts lottery rules state that winnings are payable over twenty years. "In March, I will be 95 years old. Do you realize that?" she mused to a reporter. "Ninety-five in March. Now, you know I'm not going to live twenty years."

Sure enough, with the help of attorney James Dilday of Boston, Outing sued the Massachusetts State Lottery Commission, seeking a court order that it pay her the full amount of her winnings immediately.

"She is guaranteed a twenty-year annuity with a net payment of $198,639" per year, said Joseph C. Sullivan, the executive director of the state lottery. In light of her age, he noted that any payments made after Outing's death would go to "her beneficiaries, which in this case, if needed, would be the estate."

"I would like the money so I can do what I want to do with it," Outing said. "I think I'm entitled to it. I won. So I don't understand why they don't give it to me. They took my money, so they should give me what I got. I've got plenty to do with it." She warned that if she lost her case, she would appeal. "I think it's awful the way they are treating me, just awful."

There's the case. How would you rule?

Perhaps as an accommodation to her age, the Massachusetts Superior Court heard Outing's case quite quickly. Justice Barbara A. Dortch-Okara ruled that the state lottery's rules are clear: Winnings are paid out over twenty years, and there is no cause for forcing the lottery to change things for Outing.

"I expected that," Outing said, apparently forgetting her feisty promise to appeal. "I'll make out some kind of way." Her lawyer was not as accommodating, however. "They just don't care. They're telling this woman to go take a hike."

No, they're telling Outing she's no different from anyone else. The rules are clear, and the twenty-year rule was printed on the very ticket that Outing cashed in. No one knows when they'll die, even lottery winners. To make an exception for one lucky new millionaire opens the floodgates for rule-breaking by all.

Sources:

* "Lottery Winner, 94, Sues to Get It All Now," *Boston Globe,* 29 December 2004
* "Lottery Winner, 94, Loses in Court," Associated Press, 31 December 2004

Afterword:

The "present value" of a twenty-year, $5.6 million annuity is certainly nowhere near $5.6 million, so if they were forced to pay full value immediately, the lottery would almost certainly be bankrupted, if not by this payout then by the lineup of previous winners who would want to cash in on such a ruling. Why is it reasonable to change the rules for anyone? Outing knew (or "should have known," as lawyers like to say) what the rules were when she bought the ticket. After all, that particular rule was printed *on* the ticket!

Plus, she had other alternatives. Plenty of banks would be happy to give Outing a loan, secured by the future payments. One attorney reader pointed out, "The State of Massachusetts would have a very good likelihood of making the payments as agreed. If the woman assigns the payments to the lender, payment is a virtual certainty. Most lenders would jump at the chance to make a loan that good. As attorneys, our code requires us to be 'zealous advocates of our client's best interests.' That means we must explore other avenues. Here, the other avenues were available."

We Appeal!
Some Lawyer-Readers Respond

The cases in this book were all published on the Internet, and a lot of lawyers have read them. Not surprisingly, a minority of these professional arguers sometimes try to take me on and plead that things are not as bad as they seem. I agree: They're really much worse! I am, after all, only one guy: I can't possibly find *all* the ridiculous cases that have been filed over the last few years. But I guess I can't blame them for trying.

Fisticuffs

I published a letter from a nonlawyer who wrote, "Every time I read the *Stella Awards* I can't help but roll on the floor laughing. The reality hits: *These are true*. Then I want to go out and slap some lawyer. Great job." I told the writer to be careful, since lawyers have been known to slap back. But a New Jersey attorney chose to take great exception to the comment:

> *One of your letter writers talked about going out and slapping a lawyer. You are pandering to a popular prejudice (the*

dislike of lawyers) by slanting the reporting of cases to make them appear to be frivolous. Everyone seems to hate lawyers—until they need one.

I consider it a very serious charge that I "slant" cases "to make them appear to be frivolous." While I must necessarily summarize the cases I present, I do disclose all of the sources I use so readers can read the same material for themselves—and decide if the case is being fairly represented. No one has ever presented any objective evidence that I have unfairly "slanted" my reporting.

But "New Jersey" dragged out that old consolation used by slimy attorneys everywhere: "Everyone hates lawyers—until they need one." Sorry, "Jersey": We hate them even then. Lawyers have set up a system where average people are at a complete disadvantage if they don't have someone on their side who has taken years to learn every nuance of the system—complexities that lawyers themselves have created.

The bottom line is that there *is* a problem with the abuse of civil courts in this country, but it's hard to tell how severe it is since the bad cases stand out so much. *The True Stella Awards* explores some of those cases as symptoms of a disease, and "awareness is the first step" toward curing that disease; the public must build up understanding that the problem isn't a silly case here and there, but case after case after case after case of abuse—until enough outrage builds and action becomes a must. As we see, trial lawyers whining "Everybody hates lawyers" doesn't provide much of a defense. If the public's perception of lawyers and the abuse of civil courts is wrong, it's up to *the lawyers* to fix that perception. Lawyers have graduate degrees in arguing, yet they have allowed their fellow professionals to destroy the profession's reputation until it has become universally looked upon with disrespect. The True Stella Awards was created to explore that concept from the public's point of view. The public is wrong? Then lawyers need to get to work on countering the perception. If they don't, the public will continue to simply assume that they very simply *can't* counter it.

It's Just the Way It Is

It's not just the public that is disgusted with the state of "the system"; lawyers write to ask how it can be changed too. But, they say, they feel powerless to *do* anything about it. That feeling of powerlessness starts early. A California reader says:

> *I am a law student and I love your publication. Good lawyers are about as powerless to stop the bad ones as you are. The best I can do, when I graduate, is practice ethically. Peer pressure won't stop the few bad apples from not following my example, there's too much money to make. I hope your readers someday find an opportunity to pressure their politicians for change.*

I disagree—lawyers *can* do a lot to rein in their peers; they're officers of the court, and they have a responsibility to police their ranks. It's quite understandable that no one wants to go first, but someone needs to step up; thinking about ethics is a great start. Don't sell them out, because there's more power in one voice than you think—as I'm proving. And I'm far from the only voice in this arena; the chorus is growing.

Lawyers have a duty not only to the court, but to society:

They need to keep their eyes open for frivolous cases around them and (1) *say something* when something needs to be said, and (2) *stand behind* other attorneys who boldly step up to say something! It's the classic Edmund Burke lesson: "All that's necessary for the forces of evil to win in the world is for enough good men to do nothing."

One of the nice things about outrage is it's cumulative. The outrage will build once people *really* start to understand where all those money-filled bags are coming from: our pockets. Insurance companies? Nope—where do *they* get their money? From *you*, in the form of premiums. (You *have* noticed your premiums are going up and up over the years, right?) And that's just the start. How much more does an SUV cost because a few people didn't understand they're more top-heavy than a station wagon and rolled theirs over . . . and won a big lawsuit over it? How much more do your medical visits cost not only to cover doctors' malpractice insurance, but also the unnecessary tests they order to proactively build a defense in case you sue? When people figure out how much the cost of the things they buy every day is going toward insurance and lawsuits, the outrage will grow. And grow, and grow.

Just like lawsuits have grown and grown. Trial lawyers like to say that there is no problem with lawsuits in this country, but an article in *Fortune* magazine points out that civil lawsuits soaked up 2.33 percent of the U.S. gross national product in 2002—"an all-time high, and up from 1.54 percent in 1980." Adjusted for inflation, the cost of civil lawsuits to every man, woman, and child in the country went from $87 in 1950 to $721 in 2001; it was estimated that it would reach $1,000 sometime in 2005. That makes the current lawsuit load on the classic "family of four" about $3,400 in 2004; according to the Heritage Foundation, a conservative think tank, the median federal income tax load for that family is $4,496. So understand that clearly: *Your* cost of lawsuits, reflected in your insurance premiums and the inflated cost of goods you buy, may soon be more than your federal income taxes!

Sources:

* ✶ "By the Numbers: Very Expensive Suits," *Fortune,* 19 February 2003
* ✶ "Family of Four Project," Heritage Foundation's Web site

No Such Thing as an Ethical Attorney?

Another letter from a law student, this one in New York, shows that the concept of legal ethics is a difficult one for students to ponder.

Some of your readers apparently believe there is no such thing as an ethical attorney. If, perception-wise, we have three strikes against us already the moment we pass the Bar, what possible motivation could we have to do as you have asked us so often and so eloquently to do, act as gatekeepers to the system? What else is left to do besides retreat into our own practices, act as ethically as we feel we can, and ignore all the other lawyers' behavior?

Besides the fact that ignoring unethical behavior means ignoring part of a lawyer's responsibilities as an officer of the court, doing the right thing even if you're not required to is the *definition* of ethics. Yes, lawyers have a lousy reputation, and that's largely caused by a minority of the law's practitioners. That doesn't mean you don't have a responsibility to work against that stereotype, to give the "good guys" (and I presume you intend to be part of their ranks) ammunition to repair that stereotype. Yes, lawyers are paid to put the best-looking face on the actions of their clients, but it's folly to buy into the logic that all actions *are* good.

Too, saying that you're in a no-win situation is to give in to the victimization culture. "It's not our fault! It's a stereotype! There's nothing that can be done! So we may as well ignore ethics!" It's a cliché, to be sure, but refusing to be part of the solution leaves you only one alternative: being part of the problem. Which side of that equation would your idealistic youthful self that chose to go to law school have chosen to be on? Why has that changed?

Playing with Fire

After I first published the report on people faking asbestos illnesses ("It's better than winning the lottery!" one chain-smoking industrial worker exclaimed), a lawyer in Washington wrote to complain:

> *You know, as a lawyer, I have enjoyed your good-natured poking of fun at the legal system. Particularly, I liked your ability to understand what the system was trying (albeit imperfectly) to do. But when you start extolling asbestos as an important and necessary product that is part of our history, you have lost it!!!! This product isn't the subject of numerous lawsuits because it is a Stella contender—it has killed thousands of people!!! If you think this is analogous to*

spilling hot coffee in your lap, you've jumped the tracks! Hand in your card, you're a bunch of idiots instead of a voice of reason.

Ignoring the illogic of how one guy can be a "bunch of idiots," how far does this logic go? Automobiles, for instance, have killed hundreds of thousands of people from collisions alone (forget secondary issues like pollution). That makes them "unimportant" and "unnecessary" and therefore worthy of mass lawsuits? There's a reason asbestos has been in use since ancient times: It's useful! Over its history I'll bet it has saved far more lives (e.g., protecting people from fire) than it has taken. Does that make it "safe"? That depends on your point of view—or which side of a lawsuit you're on. But like many tools and substances, it has to be used correctly or it can obviously cause harm.

Still, the safety, or lack of safety, of asbestos is *not* the issue. As I made clear in the write-up, many people have indeed been terribly harmed by asbestos, sometimes due to the extreme negligence of their employers. Such people deserve compensation. Yet because as many as 80 percent of the people who are suing have absolutely no medical problems, they are not only clogging up the system to the detriment of the people who *do* have problems, they are also helping to bankrupt the responsible companies, meaning there's nothing left for those who were truly harmed. So when an attorney comes unglued and starts in with *ad hominem* attacks and name-calling, it's rather obvious what's up: He's protecting the profit he's making from the system.

Unfortunately, I'm not "poking fun" at the legal system.

The problems are deadly serious. Yet there is so much money involved, many lawyers would have it continue as is, soaking up a greater and greater percentage of our gross domestic product until our economy grinds to a halt. They simply don't care, since their greed has blinded them to the damage we all suffer to fund their lifestyles.

Lawyers Are at <u>Such</u> a Disadvantage!

An attorney in Virginia complained:

> *One possible factor in why we lawyers tend to be held in such disrepute: When a doctor or an accountant or a plumber does something stupid, chances are no one finds out, maybe not even the client. But a lawyer's lapses in judgment are spread on the public record forever, for everyone to see. Everyone has access to our mistakes.*

Nope: I don't buy that. When doctors make mistakes, their patients often die—and most people do notice when a loved one dies. When a plumber screws up the house may be flooded, perhaps with sewage. When an accountant makes an error, the IRS often comes sniffing around. And in *all* of those cases, you know what? There will be lawyers ready to sue and make those mistakes part of the public record forever! Indeed, the legal profession has made it their business to ensure "everyone has access" to any professional's mistakes. So why should lawyers be any different? Yet they do often hold themselves up above the standards they demand of others, as the "Power Grab" later in this book shows.

"But You Proved It: The System Works!"

After reading TSA write-ups, people always want to know, "How did the case come out?" As you've read by now, even simple cases can take years to conclude. But sometimes the case write-up does have the conclusion. And just about every time that happens, I get a letter from a lawyer who writes and says something like this:

> I think this [case] demonstrates that the system actually does work. The employees filed suits, had their day in court, and a jury found that they were not entitled to compensation. This is a portrait of the American civil justice system at its finest. I suppose some would argue that these women should have never been permitted to file the suits in the first place, but if that is what you believe you might as well burn the Constitution.

The True Stella Awards isn't about a "broken" court system, just as it's not a harangue against lawyers. Just because a case is thrown out doesn't mean it's not frivolous; indeed, it's an obvious sign that it is. TSA is also not about frivolous cases succeeding; it's about the abuse of the courts, and a frivolous suit doesn't even have to make it to trial to be an utter waste of time, money, and court resources.

Yes, some parts of the system are broken, just as some of the lawyers involved are slime (and, as demonstrated, many are not). TSA is ultimately about society, and the increasing trend toward demanding compensation from someone (anyone!) for every little slight. It's about the growing something-for-nothing attitude in America that others "owe" us huge sums of money to pay for every perceived wrong. It's about an ever-growing burden on society in the form of a hidden so-called "tax" that we all pay in higher insurance premiums, reduced access to health care, and higher product costs to pay for ever-growing judgments in often ridiculous cases that clog up the courts for years, slowing down progress on righteous cases. And TSA is here to illustrate the various causes of the overall problem: It's not just the courts, the lawyers, the plaintiffs, the insurance companies, the judges, the juries, or an increasingly sick society. It's *all* of these things together— which is why virtually all attempts at "tort reform" will fail: They only address specific parts (the parts funded by monied special interests), not the whole problem. Or, if you will, minor symptoms, rather than the systemic disease.

Of course there shouldn't be prohibitions on filing suits; TSA has never argued any such thing. But we as a society must stop looking the other way when ridiculous suits are filed. We must take a stand and tell the litigants it's not right. When a truly frivolous suit is filed, there must be real and meaningful sanctions against the plaintiffs involved— and, often, their lawyers. And since the legal profession has not taken the lead in calling for such sanctions, "we the people" have only just begun to do it ourselves. Are you willing to help restore your profession's repute by joining us in that call?

ATLA "Responds" to Stella

Less than a year after the True Stella Awards went online, the American Trial Lawyers Association apparently felt some of the pressure I was applying to the issue of frivolous suits. It acknowledged my work on its Web site—

but in a rather disingenuous way. Its page, titled "Debunking Urban Legends About the Civil Justice System" (subtitle: "The OTHER Side of the Story You NEED to Hear!"), correctly pointed out that the classic years-old Winnebago "Stella Award" urban legend is false. But then ATLA's argument gets a bit, well, hazy. It concludes, amusingly citing another Web site, the urban-legend myth-busting Snopes.com:

> *In fact—bizarrely—even the self-proclaimed creators of the "Stella Award" agree that Snopes.com is right when it says the Winnebago case and its fellow "nominees" are fake! They claim they had nothing to do with the [bogus cases] e-mail currently in circulation.*

Right: The True Stella Awards Web site has had a "bogus cases" page from the very start that notes that the urban legend e-mail that has been going around for years did not originate from me. As I made clear on TSA's Web site, it's *because of* those fake "awards" that I created the True Stella Awards, since "it makes no sense to use false examples of real problems when there are so many true examples that illustrate the actual problem." But ATLA is working to cloud the issue by implying that it's "bizarre" that TSA doesn't take credit for the fake urban legend cases that have been around years longer than TSA has.

Innuendo and slurs don't advance public discussion of the very real problem of lawsuit abuse; overwhelming evidence does, and that's what TSA publishes (case after case after *case!*)—along with the sources used, so readers can review them and make up their own minds. In fact, when a reader pointed out ATLA's disingenuous wording, I linked my readers to it: I was certainly not afraid of my readers going to the ATLA site to review its wording—and again make up their own minds. Why, then, is ATLA so afraid to tell the *real* story without twisting the evidence, or even link to the Stella Awards site or the "bogus" page so people can have *all* the available facts about what's going on? They don't simply because it would quickly become obvious it's not at all "bizarre" that I had nothing to do with the silly urban legends. Rather, it would quickly become clear that trial lawyers will say anything to keep the frivolous lawsuit gravy train on track.

After I linked to the ATLA site they quickly amended the page, deleting the "bizarre" comment. But they did leave their biggest complaint of all:

> *Things like the "Stella Award" aren't just cute or harmless jabs at trial lawyers and our legal system. They clearly are part of a massive disinformation campaign designed to undermine Americans' confidence in our legal system and to benefit powerful corporate interests at the expense of average people harmed by corporate wrongdoing and indifference.*

Wow, I had no idea that I was part of a vast conspiracy to undermine the entire American legal system! I can't believe I've been missing those planning meetings! That ATLA is so scared of one guy working out of a spare room goes to show the power of putting the light of day on the cases I write up. People are getting mad, and angry Americans are definitely a major force to be reckoned with. "Things like" the Stella Awards indeed aren't "cute or harmless jabs": They're a serious effort to provoke discussion—a discussion ATLA doesn't want the country to have. "Average people" are indeed being harmed, and it's time they knew about it.

ATLA concludes on its page, "We're ALL responsible for getting the truth out." So very true; my question to ATLA, then, is, when is it going to start?

I'm Special; You Must Bow to Me

An attorney from Massachusetts wrote:

> *You are too ideologically anti-lawyer. Clearly not educated or wise. Maybe you would rather people shoot it out at high noon on High Street? Since when do you define what is appropriate for judicial determination?*

Calling me names is, as "Massachusetts" should have learned in law school, an *ad hominem* attack. Since she apparently skipped class that day and missed that question on the final, here's the definition: "appealing to personal considerations rather than to logic or reason" (*American Heritage*). That means this professional arguer didn't have a valid argument to counter the button I pushed, so she felt she had resort to feeble attempts to discredit the source.

The concept that we must either have frivolous lawsuits or shootouts in the street is pretty silly, and nicely demonstrates her own level of education and wisdom. I'm not at all "anti-lawyer"; I'm anti-stupid, whether the stupidity is committed by lawyers, plaintiffs, judges, goofballs on High Street . . . or even my own readers.

This attorney's arrogance is stunning: How *dare* a mere citizen demand to know what's going on in the country's courts and, when he sees something wrong, demand change? *We know what's good for you!* is her attitude. She forgets who she works for: The People. And we cannot have an informed opinion without seeing what's going on. It's no wonder so many lawyers don't want us to look closely: Some aspects of the system are ugly enough to cause any rational person to *demand* change, which might disrupt their money train.

Power Grab—What Lawyers Propose as "Legal Reform"

The cases presented in the True Stella Awards are typically selected to illustrate various aspects of the runaway problems in our civil legal system. The aim, over the long run, is to clearly show that there is no one aspect of the problem that needs change to "fix" the entire system; the problems are indeed systemic. It's definitely not just bad lawyers, or too many of them (though that's part of it). It's not just that the medical profession isn't weeding out bad doctors (though that's part of it). It's not just that insurance companies encourage frivolous claims and suits by making "nuisance" payments to make complainers go away (though that's part of it, too). It's not just average citizens who refuse to take responsibility for their own actions and are convinced that "someone must be to blame" for every little thing that happens to them (though that's certainly part of it!). And it's not just judges who are beholden to special interests that helped get them elected. (And that's clearly a problem.)

By demonstrating that the problem is the result of a multitude of factors, and by giving examples of real cases, TSA's purpose is to provoke thought about (and drive public discussion of) the very real impact that the lawsuit industry has on us all. Lawsuit "industry"? You bet: As discussed previously, lawsuits drained 2.33 percent out of America's gross domestic product in 2001. That's many billions more than the nation's 2001 budget for Medicare, yet lawyers still claim there's "no lawsuit problem" in this country! Even if you don't lose a lawsuit, you pay that "share" in the form of higher cost for the products you buy every day. And there's no reduction in sight.

Public discourse on the legal system is vital to getting a grasp on the issues and solving this very real and growing problem. Yet there are groups that are actively working to stop you from getting the information you need in order to be informed and make up your own mind. Indeed, they want an even larger monopoly on the practice of law.

Who would that be? The American Bar Association. The ABA seriously thinks that no one in the country should be allowed to provide any sort of legal advice to anyone unless he or she is a Bar-certified attorney.

The ABA's "Task Force on the Model Definition of the Practice of Law" proposes that each state adopt a law to codify what it means to "practice law," and that "the practice of law shall be performed only by those authorized by the highest court" of each state—attorneys. If they succeed, those state laws would be dictated word for word by the ABA.

Attorneys already dominate the legal system. Most legislators are lawyers. Most judges are lawyers. Wouldn't you like to sometimes get an outsider's perspective on what your legal rights and responsibilities might be? If the ABA gets its way, that would be illegal. Really.

Your tax preparer, real estate broker, labor union representative, credit counselor, Hollywood agent, or even your family members could be not only hit with civil fines, but even jailed for daring to give you any sort of legal advice. Help you negotiate a contract? Forbidden! Even "selecting, drafting or completing legal documents" by nonlawyers or "giving advice or counsel to persons as to their legal rights" would be *illegal* for anyone who is not a lawyer, and those who dare trespass on the lawyers' newly expanded turf could be punished with both civil and criminal penalties—which transgression will be prosecuted, of course, by lawyers.

Then-ABA president Alfred P. Carlton, Jr., claimed the proposal is simply a way to provide a "clear definition" of what the practice of law is "because there is not, in most jurisdictions, a well-understood or bright-line definition of what is and is not the practice of law." But boy, would the ABA like to draw that line! And they're working to make it so.

How far would their proposal go? "Dear Abby would be subject to prosecution every time she answered a reader's letter that dealt with a legal issue," says Thomas M. Gordon, a lawyer in Washington, D.C. And no, he's not kidding.

The U.S. Federal Trade Commission is opposed to the ABA's proposal. "We don't think it's good public policy to constrain competition in the absence of really strong evidence that the constraint has an offsetting benefit," said the FTC's deputy director of the office of policy planning, Jerry Ellig. "We haven't seen evidence of how consumers are more protected if an attorney is present."

That objection, of course, has been scorned by the ABA. "Quite frankly, [the government's objection] proceeds from the FTC's desire to assert what jurisdiction it has over the legal profession," harrumphed attorney Dudley Humphrey of North Carolina, who helped draft the ABA's proposal. The ABA's faulting the FTC for trying to protect its turf is merely an ironic example of the pot trying to call the kettle black, while conveniently ignoring that consumer protection is the FTC's very job.

Attorney Humphrey admits that real estate transactions are a driving force behind the ABA's proposal. More than 80 percent of real estate closings are accomplished without the assistance of a lawyer since only about ten states require a lawyer to complete the paperwork involved; quite naturally, when a lawyer is not required, a lawyer is rarely used. "Real estate work has been the bread-and-butter work of lawyers," Humphrey says. "It's the thing that keeps the doors open and the lights turned on. Certain elements in the real estate community, to speak quite frankly, are increasingly pressing to drive down prices."

Oh, dear! We can't have *that*, now, can we? Not when there are a lot of hungry lawyers out there ready to bill out their time at hundreds of dollars per hour to help you fill out standardized forms!

Is there truly a problem with the definition of "legal practice"? No. "There isn't too much trouble in defining law practice for lawyers appearing in courtrooms and before administrative agencies," says Professor Geoffrey Hazard of the University of Pennsylvania Law School. "The difficulty is that most of what lawyers do is office practice, and what they do in office practice is often about the same thing as lots of nonlawyer officials in companies and governments do." The ABA, he says, "is going to have a lot of difficulty with a definition that is intelligent and meaningful but not overly broad." And, he adds, that would be very difficult to do. Thus, the ABA wants to make it a legal requirement in every state that you need a lawyer to fill out forms and represent you in every negotiation, no matter whether you have the desire to be represented by an attorney or not.

The ABA's proposal is "breathtakingly broad," agrees Professor Steven Lubet of Northwestern University in Chicago. "It really reflects the worst of the profession, which is to assume that lawyers own the law and legal discourse. It's anti-democratic. In a democracy, everyone has an interest in discussing the law. The content of the law, rights and remedies, is meant to be part of the public discourse."

In addition to the FTC and Professors Hazard and Lubet—who both teach legal ethics—even many members of the ABA oppose their organization's proposal. Robert Joseph, chairman of the ABA's antitrust law section, says making legal advice from nonlawyers illegal is the wrong approach. He says lawyers should have to compete with nonlawyers, and show consumers why they do a better job at a competitive price. Huh—pretty much what used to be called the "American Way" before "gimmie gimmie gimmie" took over.

If there are too many lawyers to do the amount of actual legal work needed, the solution isn't to make more work for lawyers at the nonproductive expense of the American economy. Rather, the solution is what the rest of the economy has to deal with: "downsizing," "right-sizing," or whatever your preferred euphemism is for layoffs. That lawyers will take the sort of ridiculous cases featured in this book is already a symptom of too many lawyers. Outrageous limitations on the right to do something as simple as negotiate the terms of a contract are nothing but a pathetic attempt to grab even more power that lawyers, a class of professionals who already enjoy a gigantic monopoly, already have. As the explosion of lawsuits shows, it's time to reduce that power, not increase it at the expense of the very people the law is supposed to serve and protect.

Sources:

* "U.S. Opposes Proposal to Limit Who May Give Legal Advice," *New York Times,* 3 February 2003
* "Task Force on the Model Definition of the Practice of Law," American Bar Association, Draft Proposal of 18 September 2002

Conclusion

"What Happens" Is Really Up to You

Part 1: What Problem—Isn't Something for Nothing the American Dream?

All of these episodes add up to much more than just the abuse of the civil court system: They point to some awful truths about American society and where it is headed. Everyone, not just those sued, is damaged by runaway lawsuits. They affect our insurance rates, the cost of the goods and services we buy, and, in very fundamental ways, how we all feel about the courts and the government that runs them in the name of "we, the people."

As I noted in the introduction, I thought I would have to dig into the archives of my weird news column to find enough cases to write about, but I didn't have to: Whenever I was ready to discuss a case, I was always able to find a fresh one to write about. Can anyone *seriously* argue that the problem of frivolous lawsuits isn't increasing? And that it's not just a problem in itself, but indeed a symptom of a *much* greater problem?

That problem would be, of course, an epidemic rise in the "victim culture" in the U.S. The courts housed in the victim culture entertain cases from people who actually believe that McDonald's "forced" them to eat eighty Big Macs per week for years on end, and that had McDonald's merely informed them, "That isn't exactly healthy, sir!" they wouldn't have chowed down so many burgers, wouldn't have grown to be 385 pounds, and wouldn't be suffering from diabetes and heart disease. And dammit, that *entitles* that poor, poor victim to *compensation!* Eighty-bagillion dollars will *make him whole*, thank you! Yeah, right. McDonald's is in the business of selling a certain class of food to the people who want it. Love them or hate them, it's *your* choice whether to eat there. And shouldn't it be?

But according to the crybaby logic of people who literally are pressing such a case, McDonald's should have said, "Hey, mister, yer kinda tubby—maybe you should lay off these megafatpills for a while, like your doctor has been telling you to do for the last decade." You bet: Then they'd sue because Big Bad McDonald's was discriminating against them!

If I heat up a bowl of chili in my microwave and end up getting a steam burn when I take it out, who's at fault? (A) The microwave manufacturer? (B) The bowl manufacturer? (C) Hormel, because they didn't put a warning on the can? The victim culture's answer: (D) All of the above. My answer: (E) It's my *own* damned fault, because I'm either an idiot or I wasn't paying attention while doing something dangerous (handling *very* hot food with my bare hands). And yes, it *did* hurt, but I have a brain and managed to learn from my mistake.

Does this make sense to you? If so, don't just nod; *talk about it with others*. Use this book to start a discussion. Reading one case to them won't solve this major, complicated issue that threatens our entire economy and society, but seeing real example after real example? Ah, what power that gives! They'll see there is case after case after case, with new ways of looking at what we've all been rolling our eyes over for years. Your voice is important. Use it. I certainly don't claim that this book has the whole solution, but if enough of us cry *"Stop!"* the politicians and courts *will* listen.

So far, politicians and legal associations have proposed Band-Aid solutions that simply *will not work*. This is not a problem of a small segment of the system. Putting a cap on damages, for instance, is a Band-Aid; it does not address the real problem, which is a systemic cultural cancer. And lawyers? The American Bar Association literally thinks the way to fix the world is to require lawyers for everything, to deny citizens the right to even discuss legal issues.

A systemic problem needs a systemic solution. It won't be easy, or pretty, and it must cross multiple, and competing, barriers, but if you think the solution is a mess, consider what no solution will bring: ever-increasing litigation until every aspect of life is controlled by the government or, worse, the legal profession.

So indeed the "victim culture" is partly to blame, but there are plenty of other factors in the mix, too:

The Loss of the "Reasonable Man Doctrine"

In the past, the question to be decided was usually what a "reasonable man" would do in a given situation. It seems that there are few reasonable men left, and they're not available for courtroom duty. Instituted in common law, the reasonable person (to bring it to more modern terms) was a supposedly objective adult individual who, with typical knowledge, education, and experience, would know right and wrong, in the broad sense.

If a reasonable person would understand it's dangerous to use a metal pole to remove debris from a power line, then a lawsuit filed by a moron (or, more realistically, his survivors) who electrocuted himself doing just that would fail—presumably immediately. Today, however, such lawsuits proceed to trial if the metal pole didn't have a prominent warning sticker on it pointing out the danger that should be obvious to any "reasonable" adult.

One of the drawbacks of what seems "reasonable" may only seem reasonable in hindsight. A cop who shot an unarmed suspect might be considered negligent on its face. But if the suspect had a crowbar, was crazed from PCP abuse, was six-foot-ten and three hundred pounds versus a cop who was five-ten and one hundred sixty-five pounds, who was already down after being hit by that crowbar, then "reason" takes on a whole different light. So the "reasonable person" must be an informed person, and have at least some expertise in the subject at hand (such as police work) to actually be of use. So both sides in a case will try to spin "reason" for their own uses, for instance by bringing in supposed experts with competing points of view, which has the effect of making the "Reasonable Man Doctrine" a complicating factor, rather than a clarifying one.

This is especially true in cases of professional malpractice, such as medicine. What one expert doctor would consider quackery might be perfectly reasonable patient care practice to the one who was there: The doctor who saw the patient's symptoms, reactions to ordinary treatment, state of mind, or other factors.

So what's the result of such complications in the doctrine? Companies—and, increasingly, individuals—must take *unreasonable* precautions to guard themselves against *unreasonable* lawsuits filed by *unreasonable* people. And they have to do it with a straight face, since their very survival is at stake.

The American Dream: Something for Nothing

Americans have a strong sense of competition—it's "us against them," and there is nowhere that's more adversarial, with clear lines between the "us" and the "them," than in court. And so often it's a case of the little guy against Goliath, otherwise known as the underdog against the big corporation. Americans love to root for the underdog, no matter whether the underdog is completely responsible for his own predicament.

And why not? After all, big companies can "afford it"— and they have insurance for that kind of thing anyway, right? People feel sorry for the underdog, who may even have actual injuries, physical or otherwise. We can all relate to him, since we've all made mistakes before, and we probably will in the future; if we scratch his back, someday it might be our turn to have our back scratched. Isn't that *why* they have insurance?

Yet after awarding a few million bucks to someone who didn't read the directions and got hurt, we go home and open the mail—and rail about yet another increase in our insurance rates. *Those bloodsuckers!* we scream, and then we find out the power company just increased their rates, too. And that new car we've been saving up for? We'll never have enough, because the price goes up year after year. Rather than see the obvious cause and effect, our thoughts turn toward that "lucky" guy who won the lawsuit. If only we could get something for nothing, too!

It's a trap. The hundreds and hundreds of lawsuits add up. Yes, most of the cases are legitimate cases, perhaps even the vast majority. But the ever-increasing pace of both will inevitably bust the bank. The load has already grown to 2.33 percent of America's gross national product, up from 1.54 percent in 1980. With the cost of lawsuits likely to soon exceed the total income of individual federal income taxes, there's certainly no "something for nothing" involved in lawsuits.

So Who Is to Blame?

It's easy to blame lawyers for the problem. It's also wrong. Sure, some lawyers must take the blame for bringing frivolous suits to court in the first place. But so do the judges who give ridiculous cases the time of day, rather than tossing them out. Insurance companies are to blame, too, for rewarding outrageous behavior: They far too often pay off plaintiffs with dubious claims rather than fighting them, since they don't want to risk an even bigger payout from a sympathetic jury. Which, of course, brings us to juries: Hey, it's not our money! The big corporations can afford it, darn them! Which brings us to the "something for nothing"—and the "it may be my turn later"—mentality.

So while it's the plaintiffs who must take final responsibility, there's plenty of blame to go around.

Good Web Sites for More Information

American Tort Reform Association: www.ATRA.org
California Anti-SLAPP Project: www.CASP.net
Manhattan Institute Center for Legal Policy:
www.manhattan-institute.org/html/clp.htm
Overlawyered: www.Overlawyered.com
RAND Institute for Civil Justice: www.rand.org/icj/
And, of course, the True Stella Awards: www.StellaAwards.com

Part 2: OK, So There's a Problem—How Can It Be Fixed?

It would take at least an entire book to talk about what could be changed; the various approaches I discuss below are necessarily brief and don't cover all the approaches possible. The point, then, is to demonstrate that the solution will necessarily be very complex; don't let the tort reform crowd tell you how easy it would be "if only you fixed this one little thing"—that's their way of revealing they have a special interest behind them that wants that "one little thing" fixed because it will benefit that interest. It will take much more than "one thing" to fix the problem.

Some of the reforms discussed here have already been adopted in some states. For instance, "joint and several liability" reforms are on the books to at least some extent in several states. But no state has addressed all of these reform ideas.

Loser Pays

Concept: Whoever loses the lawsuit has to pay the legal expenses of the winning party.

When such a system is in place, the plaintiffs must have great confidence in the strength of their case to risk proceeding.

Problems: Opponents like to say such a scheme "reduces access to the courts," especially by poor people. How? If you sue a corporation, for instance, it could throw huge legal teams at the suit, running up gigantic bills. The longer the case goes on, the bigger those bills become, adding to the risk on the other side. It's a valid concern: A million-dollar legal bill is an irritant to a huge corporation, but is very likely to bankrupt a family who may have already suffered a real loss.

One way to reduce the negative effects of the "loser pays" rule is to invoke it only when a formal settlement offer is rejected.

Jury Reform

Concept: Juries are generally very good, but in some cases they need more power. In other cases, they need to be reined in.

In some ways, juries need more power: For instance, they must be able to ask questions; they are not allowed to in many states. Being able to ask questions makes them more involved in the process throughout the trial; it gives them more of a sense of responsibility since they're part of what's going on.

In other ways, juries must be reined in: Some have been known to award outrageous amounts of money when they become emotionally involved in the injury to the plaintiff. They need firm guidelines on how to award damages: see "Noneconomic Damages."

Judicial Reform

Concept: Reduce conflict of interest by appointing judges, not electing them.

Many lawyers would much rather their cases be heard by juries than by judges alone; in many states judges are elected—they run for office, and who contributes to their political campaigns? Large corporations and lawyers, setting up the possibility for conflict of interest down the road. Patronage is not the way to justice.

So how are judges then made to be responsive to the citizens they serve? While not elected, they should still be subject to impeachment by the body that appointed them, and perhaps also via recall by voters.

Noneconomic Damages

Concept: Cap "subjective" damages that cannot be proven.

"Actual" damages are those the plaintiff can prove—the plaintiff has medical bills, or damaged property, and can show what it would or did cost to repair the damage. So juries have clear guidelines on how much they can pay out to compensate plaintiffs for such damages.

But how does one put a price on "noneconomic" damages, such as pain and suffering, mental anguish, loss of consortium, and the like? Certainly a jury has no way to objectively judge such things. Guidelines should be established so juries can compensate for such losses reasonably.

Problem: This is the most-touted "reform" and is often considered the only reform needed. It allows big companies to move on and not worry about awards of hundreds of millions of dollars. But as you can see, there are plenty of other ideas to consider to create a more comprehensive solution.

Punitive Damages

Concept: Limit punitive damages, and don't let the plaintiffs get them.

There are several types of monetary damages that can be awarded in a lawsuit, such as actual or "compensatory" damages (such as medical expenses), noneconomic damages (such as pain and suffering), and punitive damages. Punitive damages essentially are a punishment to the defendant for doing wrong—a fine that is meant to put the defendant on notice not to do such a thing again so that society does not suffer further damage.

Punitive damages should be reserved for cases of actual malice or criminal negligence on the part of the defendant. In the Derrick Thomas case ("End Run," page 272), for instance, only punitive damages could explain the plaintiff's attorney begging for $100 million or more from the deep pockets of General Motors, but there was no hint of criminal negligence on GM's part: The SUV's roof exceeded federal standards even though it wasn't even required to meet those standards—the vehicle was exempt from them. Where was the criminality?

So if the government, in the guise of the court, is levying a fine on a company or other defendant for wrongdoing, why in the world does the plaintiff get the money? Or, indeed, the plaintiffs' lawyers, who generally get a big per-

centage of it? When they are warranted, punitive damages
should be paid to society—"the people"—so they can be
used to benefit society, not to unreasonably enrich plaintiffs and lawyers.

Absolute Liability

Concept: Common sense must return to product liability cases.

Product liability laws protect consumers from unsafe
products. The concept of "absolute" or "strict" liability
holds manufacturers liable for injuries caused by their
products. That sounds reasonable on the face of it, but
this doctrine actually makes manufacturers liable for *any*
injury related to their products no matter what—even if
no "reasonable person" could foresee an injury from that
product. If a someone *misuses* a product and causes injury, why should the manufacturer be liable for that
injury? A good example is the metal pool skimmer pole
that the attorney used for another purpose: to get debris
out of a power line ("Hindsight, of Course, Is a Marvelous
Thing," page 69). That's not a reasonable use for a metal
pole made for pool skimming.

Manufacturers would still, of course, be liable for injuries caused by defective products, or even from injuries
from proper use that a reasonable person could foresee—
common sense should prevail.

Joint and Several Liability

Concept: Make defendants liable only for the damages
they caused.

Lawyers love to name any possible at-fault party to a

suit, no matter how peripherally they may be involved—
each defendant is "severally liable" for the entire judgment in many states. How else do you explain the rash of
lawsuits against the radio station that carried paid ads for
a concert at a nightclub that then caught fire ("Smoke
Gets in Your Eyes," page 80)? The reason the lawyers do it:
deep pockets. Since, for instance, so many people died in the
nightclub that its insurance won't pay out enough to cover
everyone, the lawyers are trying to involve anyone else that
might have money. That way, if those peripheral companies
are judged even 1 percent at fault, they can be liable to pay
out as much as 100 percent of any reward, thanks to this
principle. It's hardly reasonable, and big corporations are
not the only victims of this ridiculous legal concept.

If a company is only partially at fault, it should only
have to pay the judged percentage of awarded damages.
Taking deep pockets out of the picture will force lawyers
and plaintiffs to more realistically judge the merits of
their case, and will drastically cut down on frivolous suits.

Secret Settlements

Concept: Once a case is brought to "the people" for
judgment, "the people" should be able to know what was
done in their name.

Once a case gets into the courts, it should stay in the
public record. If people are using government courts (you
remember the government: It's "of the people, by the
people, and for the people," which means we "own" the
courts), "the people"—all of us—should be able to know
how and why we're being used. What are the courts
ordering in our name? An "open government" should be
just that.

A secret settlement allows both sides to walk away without losing face—each can hint they got the better end of the deal. If defendants think they are doing well and would prevail, they might offer a small sum to get the case over with—it would quickly stop bad publicity, and it would cost them far less than paying the lawyers to continue on toward even a successful conclusion. The plaintiffs, knowing their case was going poorly, get to walk away looking good in the public eye since they can imply that the money award they got is an admission that the defendant did them wrong.

On the other hand, maybe the jury is clearly getting outraged at the defendants, and their lawyers think they might lose. As more facts come out, they could look worse and worse to the jury—and the public. The publicity damage could be incredible, and the defendants might find it cheaper to pay off the plaintiffs with a large sum. By keeping the amount secret, they might figure they would be less likely to attract other people with a grudge wanting to sue. Think, here, of the Firestone tire/Ford Explorer fiasco, where the tires on Explorers were implicated in a series of accidents, some fatal: In a secret settlement, an injured party may "win," but the millions of other people riding on potentially dangerous tires would not know of their risk. That obviously wouldn't serve the public interest.

Either way, such secret settlements are an abuse of the civil courts. In a lawsuit, the plaintiffs and defendants are asking the court—the tribunal branch of the government "of the people"—to judge the case and enforce that judgment. By bringing it to the public sphere, the case becomes public. Once a case has been brought into the public sphere, the case should be required to stay public.

Don't reward frivolous actions by hiding the plaintiffs' loss. By the same token, if it's not a frivolous case, allowing a guilty party to keep its guilt private is outrageous: Others who have been harmed should know what evidence has been presented so that guilty corporations can be brought to justice by all the parties that they harmed.

You want to use the people's courts to get justice? Fine, that's what they're there for. But if you want the people to enforce justice, all of the people should have a right to know the outcome of the action. The settlement should be part of the open court record for anyone to see. It can easily be enforced by making it a procedural rule: Once a suit is filed, any settlements must be presented to the court before the case can be dropped. Since there are two sides to the settlement, there would have to be a conspiracy between the two sides to violate the rule—a crime few lawyers would be willing to commit. I hope.

Venue Shopping

Concept: Limit the ability to file cases in courts known to favor a certain type of plaintiff or to disfavor a certain type of defendant.

Ask any defense attorney if there are counties where they wouldn't want to defend a suit, and you'll get an immediate answer: Yes. And the trial lawyers know those places, too; they love to file cases in jurisdictions they know to be generous with their awards. This is especially done in class-action cases.

In February 2005, President George W. Bush signed the "Class Action Fairness Act," which addresses the main concern over class-action cases: venue shopping. The law makes it easier to move class-action cases to federal court, away from friendly local juries. Consumer groups called the measure "anti-consumer" and a "major victory for big-business Republicans," while the president called it "a model of effective, bipartisan legislation." Even with a Republican president and a Republican-controlled Congress, Bush noted it took "several years" to get the legislation passed, showing how hard it is to enact effective systemic reforms to the legal system.

Class-Action Reforms

Concept: Interstate conflicts must be heard in federal courts.

When the "class" of plaintiffs comes from more than one state, the cases should be heard in federal, not state or local, courts. This keeps lawyers from filing cases in specific jurisdictions where the juries are known to be generous with the money of out-of-state deep pockets.

Also, there need to be limits on what the attorneys' share of the take is when they win class-action cases. Often, the lawyers get huge rewards while the actual members of the class get coupons on a future purchase— or less. The Home Depot case ("Forget the Price, What's the Cost?" page 172) illustrates this sort of thing nicely.

Rule Changes

Concept: Lawyers can be blindsided by their clients.

Some attorneys end up in situations in which they take a case, then discover through investigation that the claims are frivolous. In many states, ethics rules say they can't drop out of the case—they're committed to continue on with their client even though they don't think the case has merit. That needs to change.

Rule 11

Concept: There's a rule against frivolous motions, but it's rarely used.

In federal courts there is Rule 11, which allows one side to ask for sanctions against the other side for acting frivolously. It's rarely used, since if there is any chance of getting even, the other side will try—the opposing counsel will often make a Rule 11 motion to counter the other side's Rule 11 motion, leaving the court with a catch-22 squabble over the rules, rather than hearing the arguments in the case.

Court rules need to be clarified, and frivolous uses of Rule 11 must be punished, no matter which side brought it up. The bottom line: Just enforcing the rules on the books would help a lot to stem abuse, especially if their use and abuse is made more clear.

Certificate of Review

Concept: "Experts" often are not.

A certificate of review is needed in many states to show that a "qualified expert" has reviewed the case and agrees it has merit. But the "expert" can be anonymous, meaning that there is no review of the review. There's nothing to keep the lawyer from just stating that an "expert" has reviewed the case, so many lawyers simply lie about the review. More often, of course, they simply hire any crackpot who has a grudge and is willing to say that there is a case.

The defendant must have the ability to cross-examine the "expert" who certified the case in the first place.

Avoidance Is Saying You're Sorry

Concept: Allow human decency.

Some states have actually had to pass laws saying lawyers cannot use a simple apology as evidence of wrongdoing, because that's exactly what they were doing. It's not in the best interest of a civil society to not be able to say "sorry" when something goes wrong, whether or not the person or organization involved did anything wrong. It's reasonable for a doctor to tell a patient that he's sorry he can't do more to help her; it doesn't mean he committed some sort of malpractice. So why isn't such a simple, humane rule the law in every state? It needs to be.

And Last, Society Must Take a Stand

Ultimately, this is the most important "reform" that can take place: We as a society must stop looking the other way when ridiculous suits are filed. We must take a stand and tell the litigants it's not right. When a truly frivolous suit is filed, there must be real and meaningful sanctions against the plaintiffs involved—and, often, their lawyers.

When I said that online, a reader replied,

> *In principle, I agree completely. In practice, I really have no idea how to have any real impact on the situation. You are doing an admirable job of spreading the word about the problem, but I lack your skills in this particular department. I have told friends about my own Stella Award–style encounter with the court system. As you might expect, they all*

commiserate and say how bad things are, but that doesn't really change anything. I have personally talked two people out of suing in the past, so maybe that is a help, but a really tiny one if so. Do you have any concrete suggestions for what we 'ordinary, nonlawyer citizens' can do to really change the system?

The reader didn't grasp that he had done *exactly* what needs to be done. He talked to others about his own legal situation and theirs. He listened to the stories of more than one person and then gave his opinion about their "cases," and ended up talking two people out of filing frivolous suits. That is, indeed, just what I am talking about: Keep your ears open, find out what others are thinking, and give your opinion. Sometimes the advice will be, "Yeah, you were really wronged! I agree that if they don't make it right, you should sue." And that's OK: That's what the courts are there for. But when they're saying their son was speeding through a snowstorm and not wearing a seat belt, and they're thinking about suing for $100 million, as Derrick Thomas's mother did, you have a priceless opportunity to tell them what you think of their contemplated action. You don't have to create a publication or make speeches. Grassroots efforts like that are in fact very, very effective—as the reader found out.

Now, imagine expanding that to every reader of this book. Then expand it again, to every citizen with common sense. Imagine all of those people telling their political representatives that the system is broken and we expect them to fix it—or we'll elect someone who will.

That is when things will really start to change. Effective reform of the people's courts is necessarily up to us all.

Appendix:

Annual Award Winners and Runners-up

2002

#7: Philip Shafer, who sued over having to sit next to a "huge man" on an airline. *"Mommy, He's Touching Me!,"* page 133.

#6: Deanna Brown Thomas and Yamma Brown Lumar, who demanded royalties for "helping" write songs for their father, singer James Brown, when they were as young as three. *"I Said Now, Daddy!,"* page 227.

#5: Robert Paul Rice, who sued the Utah prison system since it wouldn't let him practice his "Vampire" religion in his cell. *"I Vant to Suck Your Vallet,"* page 160.

#4: Kathleen Ann McCormick, who sued her doctors for not *forcing* her to follow their health advice. *"Nah Nah Nah Nah (I Can't Hear You!) Nah Nah Nah Nah,"* page 46.

#3: Bob Craft, who legally changed his name to Jack Ass—and then sued the *Jackass* TV show and movie for disparaging his good name. *"If the Name Fits . . . ,"* page 278.

#2: Hazel Norton, who sued her doctor because "I might get a couple thousand dollars," even though she admits she was not harmed. *"Unwanted Side Effects,"* page 183.

Winner: Sisters Janice Bird, Dayle Bird Edgmon, and Kim Bird Moran sued their mother's doctors because they had to witness the doctors try to save their mother's life. *"NIED Given Dose of Common Sense,"* page 48.

2003

#8: Stephen Joseph, who sued Oreo cookies in a publicity stunt. *"Trans-Frivolous Lawsuit,"* page 23.

#7: Shawn Perkins, who sued over a classic "act of God"—being hit by lightning. *"I See the Light!,"* page 96.

#6: Caesar Barber, who sued fast-food chains since it was their fault he was obese and ill—they "made" him eat their food! *"And the McBandwagon Plays On,"* page 72.

#5: Cole Bartiromo, who sued his school for not letting him play baseball. *"Whiff!,"* page 199.

#4: David Hanser, a pedophile priest who sued his victim. *"SLAPP Him Around,"* page 258.

#3: Wanda Hudson, who hid—and sued when no one came looking for her. *"The Countess of Monte Cristo,"* page 62.

#2: Doug Baker, who spent $20,000 to find his lost dog, and sued the dog-sitter. *"A Dog-Eat-Dog World,"* page 222.

Winner: The City of Madera, California, which sued a police equipment supplier after one of its police officers mistook her sidearm for a Taser—and shot a handcuffed suspect to death by accident. *"A Stunning Situation,"* page 93.

2004

#6: The Tribune Company, which sued one of its newspaper carriers after the company screwed up his payroll. *"Payday Play,"* page 261.

#5: Sharper Image, which got a bad review from a consumer magazine, and sued to shut them up. *"A Sharp SLAPP in the Face,"* page 237.

#4: Edith Morgan, who sued the auto manufacturer after her son crashed his car—speeding in a snowstorm while not wearing a seat belt. *"End Run,"* page 272.

#3: Tanisha Torres, who sued because the name of her town was spelled in a joking way on her cell phone bill. *"It Ought to Be a Crime,"* page 120.

#2: Mortgage lender Homecomings Financial, which allowed identity thieves to steal a customer's account—and then sued the victims. *"We've Got Your (Account) Number, Chump,"* page 248.

Winner: Mary Ubaudi, who, after being in a car accident, sued Mazda since it "failed to provide instructions regarding the safe and proper use of a seat belt." *"Click-It or Ticket,"* page 109.

Index

Acknowledgments

A lot of people stand behind the author of a book, and they deserve acknowledgment. In my case, my wife, Kit, has to come first: She hated the idea of my taking on Yet Another Project, but she understood my passion for wanting to bring more justice and common sense to the legal system, and my desire to further the dialogue in the public arena by providing real cases to discuss, rather than the urban legend stories people usually pass around.

My agent Andrew Stuart knew this was a book that needed to be widely read, and is largely responsible for it being placed with a publisher big enough to handle it and promote it effectively.

Dutton and my editor there, Mitch Hoffman, had the guts to let this book exist. It helped that his boss, editorial director Brian Tart, was already a fan of the True Stella Awards when my agent sent him the proposal for this book, which is further proof of the enormous power of publishing on the Internet. Both had excellent suggestions for explaining some of the arcane topics covered in a way that would be entertaining as well as informative. Then Dave Cole, the nitpicking grammarian copy editor, got hold of the manuscript and helped to make the text consistent, less confusing, and even easier to understand, as well as catching my typos and other silly errors. We left one typo as a mental exercise for the reader. Let us know if you find it.

Virginia Norey designed the book, Tonya Goodnow created the award graphic, and Dave Casler took the author photo.

Jeffrey Anbinder, a True Stella Awards reader—and recent graduate of the Benjamin N. Cardozo School of Law in New York City—assisted with some of the legal research, in many cases finding the obscure filings that allowed me to tell you what happened at the end. When possible, he helped me learn and report the conclusion.

Last, and very importantly, is my online readership: I present the True Stella Awards' tens of thousands of online subscribers with the case write-ups and, because they can easily e-mail me, they do—they tell me what is wrong with my arguments, point out flaws and weaknesses, and propose counterarguments. Their ongoing critiques of what I publish online have helped me refine my points, so that what you finally get here has been improved dramatically over what I published online. Thus this book is far more, and far better, than a simple reprinting of the cases I published on the Internet over the last few years.

My thanks to you all.

Randy Cassingham
Ridgway, Colorado

About the Author

Randy Cassingham has a degree in journalism, but he never wanted to be a conventional news reporter. His boundless sense of curiosity has led him to explore a number of careers, including commercial photographer, free-lance writer (including magazine articles, technical articles, fiction, and screenplays), publisher, ambulance paramedic, search-and-rescue sheriff's deputy, process engineer, business consultant, and a technical publisher and software designer at NASA's Jet Propulsion Laboratory. He is an expert on using the Internet to reach a diverse international audience with entertaining human interest content, and publishing and distribution on the Internet. His online column at ThisIsTrue.com is one of the largest subscription features on the Internet, with readers in more than 200 countries. He also created StellaAwards.com to explore the implications of runaway lawsuits. He and his wife, Kit, live in rural western Colorado, where both are volunteer first responders to emergency calls.